Contents

Acknowledgements
This book is dedicated to my two crazy, kind and loving children of whom I am infinitely proud.

I am grateful to my husband for his constant support and encouragement and to my mother-in-law who has helped us more than we can thank her for, and who might now believe that it's a "real book".

Thank you to Hedi Argent for her patience, enthusiasm and belief and for making a life-long dream of writing a book come true.

About the author
Jayne Lilley was born in the Midlands in 1972. She spends her time being mum to two children, one by birth and one through adoption, being wife to Dan and working in a finance department. In her spare time she meditates, enjoys Spanish red wine and Italian food. This is her first book.

The Our Story series

This book is part of CoramBAAF's Our Story series, which explores adoption and fostering experiences as told by adoptive parents and foster carers.

Also available in the series:
- *Flying Solo* by Julia Wise
- *In Black and White* by Nathalie Seymour
- *Adoption Undone* by Karen Carr
- *A Family Business* by Robert Marsden
- *Together in Time* by Ruth and Ed Royce
- *Take Two* by Laurel Ashton
- *Holding on and Hanging in* by Lorna Miles
- *Dale's Tale* by Helen Jayne
- *Frozen* by Mike Butcher
- *When Daisy met Tommy* by Jules Bell
- *Is it True you have Two Mums?* by Ruby Clay
- *As if I were a Real Boy* by Gordon and Jeannie Mackenzie
- *Becoming Dads* by Pablo Fernández
- *Finding our Familia* by Stevan Whitehead

The series editor

Hedi Argent is an established author and editor. Her books cover a wide range of placement topics; she has written several guides and story books for young children.

1

How it all began

UP TO JANUARY 2012

Adopting our second child was an easy decision to make. My husband Dan and his brother Ian were adopted as babies and I've known my stepdad as my dad since I was in my late teens. It doesn't matter that we aren't all related by "blood" to our parents – they are our family. They pick you up when you are down and celebrate with you when you are happy, they care for you and are there for you when you need them; where does "blood" come into that?

Dan and I already had a four-year-old little boy together called Charlie. We'd been dating for two years when we made the decision to have children, and I became pregnant three months later. It was a crossroads in life for me: I was 34 years old and had just been promoted to manager of a large finance team. I'd worked incredibly hard for a number of years and, sadly, I allowed my job to define me. It was like an all-consuming obsession. I'd been financially independent for some time but with this promotion I felt like I'd finally got the recognition I craved.

When I met Dan, I was a career woman living in a luxury apartment in the city close to where I worked. I enjoyed the finer things in life and could afford them – a far cry from my humble beginnings.

My birth father left the family home after meeting a Sunday school teacher at an Open University summer school. He soon moved from our council house to live with his mistress and her three young sons in a leafy middle class area about ten miles away; I was thirteen and my sister was seven. During my childhood, my father rarely worked; the only job that I remember him having was when I was very young. After being made redundant, he was unable to find work and claimed benefits until he left the family. He became depressed and was emotionally unavailable for many years, so I didn't feel like he left a father figure-sized gap in my life. But his departure did leave us in a state of poverty. He didn't contribute to our upbringing, always prioritising his new family over the one he'd left behind. It was very difficult for me to visit his new "middle class life" with his three stepsons, especially as I would return to literally nothing. The food cupboards were often empty, electricity and gas were frequently disconnected and we'd have to sit huddled in blankets with candles. During this very difficult time, my mum re-educated herself at college and got the first job that she applied for. She did her best, but once employed, all her benefits stopped and we didn't seem to be any better off financially. As a young teenager I did what I could, taking babysitting jobs, having paper rounds and helping with the housekeeping while my mum worked. Once I reached eighteen, I told my father that I didn't want any further contact with him. He was still not contributing to my sister's upkeep and was completely unreliable. It had come to a head for me when he invited my sister to live with him, but when she agreed and told my mother, he changed his mind and told her she couldn't come. That sort of thing had happened time and time again and I had to deal with the emotional fall-out from his broken promises. I've neither seen nor spoken to him since that day twenty-five years ago.

Dan and I worked for the same company and met each other on a work's night out. We dated casually for over a year before Dan asked me to move in with him as a "lodger". He owned a three-bedroomed house and rented two rooms to friends – one of them had decided to move in with his girlfriend, leaving a room spare. It was an ideal situation – we were living together but I had my own room to escape to when either of us wanted a bit of time out.

Dan's upbringing was in direct contrast to mine – he and his brother were adopted when they were only a couple of weeks old. They were both what is known as "relinquished", so their birth mothers were either very young or had decided that this was the best option for their babies. Children at risk of abuse or neglect were not as often removed from their parents as they are today. Dan and Ian were always told that they were adopted, and had Dan wanted to look for his birth parents, his mum, Jean, and dad, Brian, would have done all they could to help. They lived a financially comfortable and stable life with Brian working hard to start his own welding factory, which became a great success. Dan adored his dad, and his mum often talks of how Dan would be his dad's little shadow, and how like him Dan is in both temperament and mannerisms. When Dan was in his mid-twenties, his dad tragically died. Jean and Brian were due to fly out to Australia for an extended holiday and on the morning of the flight Brian was taken ill and sadly passed away in hospital the next day. Jean, Dan and Ian's world was ripped apart. Family weddings, the births of grandchildren and any subsequent celebrations would be tinged with the sadness that Brian wasn't a part of them. After losing his father, Dan lived according to the motto that "life is too short"; he didn't want to waste it as he was acutely aware that life can change direction in an instant.

Dan and I were both of a similar mind-set when we met each other: neither of us needed a partner in their lives but we enjoyed each other's company and got on well and gave each other space to see where our relationship might lead, and in time it led to a discussion about having children together.

My pregnancy with Charlie was perfect. I didn't suffer from morning sickness or any pregnancy-related ailments. My job required travelling to France occasionally and I was able to do this right up until the 30th week of pregnancy because I just felt so fit and healthy. Around this time, Dan surprised me with a trip to Madrid on Valentine's Day where he proposed, and I agreed to marry him, in the Botanical Gardens. Life was good.

At 9.32am on Sunday 18 May, I saw my beautiful Charlie's face for the first time. The birth was difficult and ended with an emergency caesarean but this was already a distant memory after I held him for the first time. Looking at this wonderful but helpless little boy I knew that my life had changed forever and nothing was as important to me as loving him and keeping him safe; my priorities changed from that moment on.

I left the job that I'd worked so hard for; it didn't give me the same satisfaction after having Charlie. I wanted to be with him as much as I could before he started school. I spent the next few years working on temporary part-time assignments and spent precious time with my son, watching him grow into a loving and confident little boy. The hope that I'd soon be pregnant again was never far from our minds.

We only wanted a small age gap between Charlie and any brothers and sisters but this didn't seem to be happening. Three was our magic number – the number of children we wanted to complete our little family. We wanted two birth children and to adopt a third; we'd always talked about adoption and it was incredibly important to Dan, so we had discussed it quite early on in our relationship. It was always a given that we would try to adopt at some point – Dan wanted to pay tribute to his mum and dad by giving a child the same start and loving family that they gave to him. I wanted to have as many children as I could, and I couldn't see that I would love an adopted child any differently to one I had given birth to.

Looking forward to the start of 2012, Dan and I accept the fact that it doesn't seem as though a second child is going to come along for us any time soon and that maybe the time is right to look further into the prospect of adopting sooner rather than later. I think about this for a few weeks and agree with Dan. I've heard that the adoption process is lengthy and that it could take around two years to complete. That would make Charlie six years old. It made the decision easy; I'd never wanted Charlie to be an only child and six already seems old for him to be introduced to his first brother or sister.

I tell Dan that I agree with him and that the time is right. We should find out what we can about adopting.

2

The wrong turn

JANUARY 2012–JUNE 2013

Not people to hang around once we've made a decision, we find that there is an adoption information evening at a local hotel on Wednesday 18 January. I call the agency running the event and book us two places. We didn't really want to tell anyone of our plans so early on in the process but we need a babysitter for Charlie; Jean, Dan's mum, will always look after him, but it's her birthday, so we have to tell her where we're going. We make her promise to keep it to herself as Dan and I aren't sure what to expect, and although we are desperate to have another child, we want to make sure that we are doing the right thing for all of us first.

Dan and I finish work and go straight to the hotel; we arrive an hour-and-a-half early but surprisingly we're not the first there! We sign in and take our seats – fortunately there's plenty of tea, coffee and biscuits to keep us going until the evening formally begins.

The room fills up steadily in the next hour or so with a mixed bunch of single men, single women and both young and middle-aged couples. I start to feel a little more relaxed and read through the leaflets telling us a bit about the agencies represented and fill in a form asking for further details about us. The Head of Children's Services for the local authority finally arrives and she begins by talking us through the types of children who are waiting for adoption; she makes it abundantly clear that the children we are eagerly waiting to adopt will all have lived through damaging experiences. She tells us that nowadays very few birth parents choose to have their babies adopted, and most of the children in care have been removed from their families due to neglect or abuse. Wow! I wasn't looking at adoption through rose-tinted glasses but to have the facts presented in this way is quite a shock to me. I think because we have Charlie and have looked after and loved him for his four years of life, it is difficult to hear that not all children have that same start.

After the talk, we have the opportunity to speak to social workers who will decide whether to take us forward to the next stage. We are allocated a social worker called Jan from a different authority to the one in which we live, and we nervously approach the desk. Jan puts us at ease and asks us about ourselves and Charlie and our motivation to adopt; after around twenty minutes of chat Jan tells us that yes, an initial interview will be arranged. We both leave the hotel feeling happy, excited and apprehensive all at the same time. We've taken the first tentative steps to adding a new son or daughter to our family.

It's difficult to get back to normal family life now that we've taken that first step; I just want to get started and I know that Dan feels the same. We've both decided to keep all of this from Charlie for now, as after the first home visit either party could decide not to go any further. At last the appointment letter comes and we're on!

Friday 9 March 2012: Initial enquiry home visit
The meeting with two social workers from the adoption agency is arranged for 9.30am. By 9am the house has been cleaned from top to bottom and we've taken Charlie to nursery. Dan is relaxed but the same can't be said for me, I pace the room for the next thirty minutes waiting for that knock on the door. There are so many thoughts and feelings going through my mind: I'm nervous about what we are going to be asked. I have had a difficult childhood and a complicated adult history – what if they say no to us? Finally they arrive at 9.30am on the dot. The two women are very pleasant and introduce themselves as Sharon and Mandy. Sharon takes charge of the meeting almost as soon as we are all seated; she explains that there are a series of questions that we will both be asked in turn and leaves it to us to decide who wants to go first. As my past is more complex, I nervously agree to be interviewed first. I figure that if they hear all I have to say and still want to question Dan, it will be a positive sign.

First I am asked about my childhood, which isn't easy to discuss. My mother struggled to cope with the debts that my father had left, and with bringing up two girls on her own. She became seriously depressed and relied on me emotionally, which for a young teenager was a huge weight of responsibility. I'm worried that I've been a little bit too honest and that this is going to ruin our chances. When I've finished speaking there aren't any comments, and we move on to the next topic: 'Past relationships' – great! Another tricky subject!

I had my first serious boyfriend in my mid-twenties; he won the lottery and very publicly left me; on the rebound, I married an alcoholic who went on to commit suicide. I retell the events candidly. I hesitatingly ask if there's anything I've said that concerns them. They say, not at all, they even feel that my resilience will help me to relate to the child we eventually adopt, as he or she will have come from a similar background. Not what I was expecting at all!

It's Dan's turn next, and he tells about his childhood and previous relationships. In contrast to the hour-and-a-half it took for my interview, his takes twenty minutes. Then the social workers move on to ask about our marital relationship, Charlie, our health, employment, our support network and our hobbies.

The two social workers seem very happy with what they've heard from us, and ask to look around the house. We show them around and they want to know if we have any building works planned for the future. We do, actually; we're planning to extend our kitchen later on in the year. Mandy and Sharon tell us that we need to have this work completed before a child can be placed with us. We have an open bannister and they tell us that this will need to be changed, as it's a health and safety risk. I explain that we've already lived in the house with a toddler without an incident, but there's no budging them.

We return to the living room and they start to wrap up the meeting. Dan and I say how we'd like three children in total, two birth children and one adopted. Sharon stops us in our tracks and tells us that if we adopt we should not have more birth children because it could make an adopted child feel the odd one out in the family, but if the adopted child's birth mother becomes pregnant again, we would probably be able to adopt that child. Dan and I look at each other in stunned silence – we can't quite comprehend what we've just heard! I hadn't realised that we would have to make an either/or decision! We're told that we need to go away and think about whether we want to adopt or have more birth children. When the social workers have left, Dan and I try to process what we have just been told. It feels like it's too big a decision to make.

We both go to work in the afternoon and I can't concentrate. In my heart I want to have one last shot at another birth child before trying to adopt. Dan and I talk later that evening and agree that we'll contact the agency and put the adoption on hold. It's not a decision that we've taken lightly; I keep thinking of all those children out there who need families, but being told that we aren't allowed to have any more birth children if we adopt has forced us to change the order in which we do things.

September 2012

Charlie, Dan and I continue our life as usual; I'm working in temporary jobs and have been lucky enough to have the six weeks' summer holiday off with Charlie. I've made the most of it and we've enjoyed day trips to museums and family holidays to UK beaches – not much sun but loads of laughter! Charlie leaves his nursery in September 2012 and moves to the reception class of the local school. I have an interview lined up for the first week in September and on the day of the interview I feel very strange and emotional. The interview goes really well. I tell Dan about my weird feelings and he immediately tells me to do a pregnancy test; there are loads of them in the bathroom cabinet because I test each month, but each month has led to disappointment. I take the test and Dan's right, I'm pregnant! The company call to offer me the job but I turn it down; it doesn't seem fair to accept a permanent job when I've just found out I'm going to be leaving in nine months' time.

Tuesday 9 October 2012

Dan and I are over the moon, this is what we've longed for, but something doesn't feel right. I know that no two pregnancies are the same, but this time I feel terrible: I'm exhausted all the time and my body is very swollen, I just know that something's wrong. Then the bleeding starts. I go to the local hospital and the doctor wants to check my hormone levels; I get a call later that evening asking me to go back to hospital as they think I might be having an ectopic pregnancy. The consultant at the hospital tells us that he wants me to stay overnight as a precaution and that they'll scan me in the morning. I'm bewildered as I'm not in any pain – this can't be an ectopic pregnancy, surely?

Wednesday 10 October 2012
It's morning and Dan comes with me for the scan. The midwife finds a heartbeat and shows us on the screen; I immediately burst into tears – I can see my little baby! The doctor comes to see me afterwards and tells me that there's a likelihood of twins as there seem to be two heartbeats! What a rollercoaster of a day! I have to go back in two weeks for another scan just to check that everything's going OK. Twins – what fantastic news!

Friday 26 October 2012
Back at the hospital again for the next scan, Dan and I are ridiculously excited now that we've got used to the idea of having twins. I've had a bit of bleeding in the two weeks since the last scan but I'm not too worried – I've read that it's normal with twins.

The midwife looks at the screen and I can tell by her face that something's very wrong. After several minutes of silence, she turns to me and says she's sorry, but there isn't a baby and would we like some time alone. I don't want to stay in that room for a minute longer than we have to, I want to speak to the doctor and know what's happened. The doctor tells me how sorry he is but that the babies are no longer living; she asks what treatment I would like to have, and recommends that we let the babies come away naturally rather than have an operation to clear my womb. I've never had an operation before so agree to the natural way. I have to go back to hospital in two weeks' time for a scan to check that everything is clear. Dan and I go home and we just walk and walk and walk. We're both devastated.

Saturday 10 November 2012

Back in hospital again for a scan, we're asked to wait in a room on our own; we don't have to sit with the expectant mothers who are clutching the beautiful photographs of the lives growing inside them. All I can think is that it's not fair. Then I think back to the adoption evening and about the children whose parents easily get pregnant but have child after child taken from them. How must that feel, and why is it so easy for them to have children, and why can't I? Dan, Charlie and I would have loved these babies so much and now they've gone, quite literally, down the drain! Life isn't fair, and I know that being negative isn't helpful but I'm just very hurt. We're ushered into the scanning room and the midwife solemnly looks at an image of my empty womb. But she turns to me and tells me that there's still some matter in there and that they need to remove it. I must return the following Saturday, essentially to have an abortion. When is this nightmare going to end?! The babies died at the end of September and we're now at the end of November! I've tried to carry on as normal for Charlie's sake. I don't want him to know how upset I am and have even got myself a new job, which I am due to start on the Monday after my next scan following the abortion.

Friday 23 November 2012

At last, the news that we want to hear – everything's now clear; life can restart. I'm going through the motions, I know, but I need routine to get me through this horrible time. A friend of mine is pregnant with her second child and her due date is around the same time that mine would have been. Although I'm delighted for her, I can't face seeing her. Yes, I'm jealous and still very raw about our drawn-out and traumatic experience. I need things to get back to normal, not just for me but for Dan and the little boy who relies on me to be his mummy. I need to focus on what I've got and not think about what might have been, but that's easier said than done. Christmas is fast approaching and we're going to Lapland on 1 December with my mother-in-law, brother-in-law, sister-in-law and niece. This is going to be a once-in-a-lifetime experience. It'll be Charlie's first time in an aeroplane and he's so excited about seeing the "real" Father Christmas.

Sunday 5 May 2013
It's my mum's 65th birthday tomorrow and she wants us to go to a National Trust house in Wales for the day to celebrate. As it's a long journey with a five-year-old, we travel down today and are meeting up with the rest of the family tomorrow. We've had other holidays with Charlie, but he hasn't stayed in a hotel before, and to say he's excited is an understatement! Last year was dreadful for us and we're all determined to make this year a good one. Being near the sea and driving through the beautiful Welsh countryside, I feel back to my old self – it's just what I need. Dan has been patient and kind as always; I know that I become withdrawn when I have something that I need to work through.

June 2013
The break in Wales was fantastic. I have come back feeling refreshed and knowing what I want from the future. I definitely want more children but I don't want to be pregnant again. Our local doctor always says: 'When the mother of a family is ill, then the whole family knows about it', and it's true: the difficult pregnancy, the repeated scans and coming to terms with the loss of the twins took its toll not only on me, but also on Dan and Charlie. I do not want any of us to go through that again.

Dan and I have talked and we have decided to contact the social workers to say that we are ready to go ahead.

3

We begin again

AUGUST 2013–DECEMBER 2013

Monday 12 August 2013
Dan and I have decided that 2013 is going to be a year when we make things happen for us. We've completed the kitchen extension and finished off all the other outstanding DIY jobs. The house is looking really good and we're pretty much back on an even keel emotionally.

Dan tells me that he's left it to me to decide our next move in my own time and that he will support whatever I want to do to increase our family. IVF isn't an option for me – I wouldn't want to put that level of stress on us all and I'm not sure if I could handle the disappointment. I've been very lucky to experience having a birth child, and I'm not concerned about my capacity to love a child who joins our family by adoption.

Dan calls the local authority and lets them know of our wish to start the adoption process again; he's told that we need to put our request in writing.

Tuesday 1 October 2013
The local authority contacted us by letter on 28 August to

tell us that the process to adopt has changed and that there are now two stages: Stage One takes approximately two months and consists of background checks and references, plus three days of training to give us more information about adoption issues and the children waiting to be adopted. Stage Two, also known as the "home study", then has to be completed within four months. It all seems very structured, with definite timescales, which is brilliant and in contrast to what I was expecting. I'd prepared myself for it to take around two years to complete the process before even thinking about a particular child. It's very encouraging to think that by April 2014, we could be talking about our new son or daughter!

An initial meeting has been set up with a social worker to check that now is the right time for us to adopt; that meeting is today and the social worker is Mandy, who visited us before. She is due at 10am and arrives promptly; Dan and I are both a little more relaxed this time as we know what to expect. Fortunately, details of our first meeting have been retained, so we only need to talk about the time since our last meeting. I tell Mandy about the miscarriage and she's keen to know how we grieved, how we worked as a family unit to come to terms with what had happened and how we see our family growing and going forward. I feel that I'm now fully committed to adopting. If I'm being totally honest, Dan was the driving force last time – I did want to adopt, but I probably also wanted to keep trying for another birth child for a while longer. Now I just want to get things moving.

Mandy is happy with what we've said and is going to recommend that we move forward to Stage One. We are told that we should receive a letter to that effect in due course.

Thursday 10 October 2013
We've received the confirmation letter and Stage One

information pack. Being a bit cynical, I expected it to take longer than the ten days it has taken – I'm absolutely delighted that we're officially now in Stage One of the adoption process! We need to have an enhanced CRB (Criminal Records Bureau) check,* complete a health questionnaire and organise a full health examination with our doctor. Mandy calls to tell us that there are spaces on the November preparation training sessions, if we're free to attend. Things really do seem to be moving quickly.

Now Dan and I discuss how we can start to include Charlie. I've broached the subject lightly by generally asking him if he'd like to have a brother or sister and, depending on his mood, it's 'Yes Mummy, I'd really like a brother,' or 'I want it to be just me, you and Daddy'. A lot of our friends have more than one child, so after visiting them we talk to Charlie about the sibling relationships between friends' children. He does seem to be warming to the idea, but as he's only five years old, Dan and I decide that we will continue to tread lightly.

Tuesday 12 November–Thursday 14 November 2013: Group training

We are lucky that the training sessions are being held close to our home. We drop Charlie off at his school breakfast club and arrive at the venue with a few minutes to spare. Neither Dan nor I are nervous about the training; we're both used to large group training sessions at work and have no problem with putting our opinions forward. I can imagine that this method of training isn't for everyone though, especially if you don't like talking in front of lots of strangers.

We're welcomed by one of the social workers leading the session and offered tea and biscuits. It seems that most of the group have already arrived and are seated, so Dan

---

* Now known as the DBS (Disclosure and Barring Service).

16

and I find chairs at the front. Looking around the room, there are eight couples and a single man. We introduce ourselves: half are white British like us and the remainder are Asian, Polish, and South American; we are a real mixed bag. Our "icebreaker" exercise is to split from our partners and work with another person to discuss what we know about our names and why our parents chose them. I'm with a Welsh/South American couple due to the odd number in the group; they are really friendly and we have quite a giggle – all in all, a good start. We're told that the training usually lasts for five days, but as the whole adoption process has changed and is shorter, the training has been condensed into three sessions and we must therefore be prepared to move from topic to topic quite quickly.

The areas to be covered in Day 1 are the more difficult ones of abuse, child development, brain development, the impact of neglect on children, loss and separation and the "adoption triangle" (the relationship between the child, adoptive parents and birth family). I don't think that any members of the group are looking forward to today's topics, but of course we need to understand what the children who will be joining our families may have experienced. The training is very interactive; we have the opportunity to splinter off into small groups to work through the topics. It's a great way to get to know the other people in the group, even if the subject matter is very dark.

Dan and I work with the couple sitting next to us; they are around our age and want to adopt a sibling group. To begin with, we're all a bit wary of contributing as I think we're all conscious that the trainers will feed back to our agencies whether we are ready to move on to the next stage. We don't have long to work through the exercises so there's not much time for small talk.

Child development is very interesting. The metaphor being used is that of a brick wall and that our children, depending on their experiences, will have certain "bricks" missing, the bricks being the milestones that most children reach at certain ages. We're told that it's very likely that our children will have developmental delay as a result of what they've experienced in early life.

During the breaks we have time to look at books and literature from BAAF* and Adoption UK; Dan and I leaf through a journal that is filled with children's smiling faces, all hoping to find their "forever families". It's incredibly sobering and brings home to me just how many children are waiting to be adopted. I can't stop thinking about all those lovely little faces and what they have already experienced in their short lives. When Dan and I get home and see Charlie, I hug him just a little bit tighter than usual.

I'm so pleased that we've attended the training course so early on in the adoption process. It has made us both more determined than ever to proceed.

13 November 2013: Day 2
It's the second day of training, and everyone is feeling a little bit jaded after yesterday's tough subject matter. Today we're looking at attachment, resilience, identity and matching. Yesterday the scenarios in the video footage were dramatised, so fortunately we didn't see any examples of real children in abusive situations, but today we watch excerpts from a Professor Robert Winston documentary that shows some disturbing examples of poor parent–child relationships, for example, a mother who can't relate to one of her young daughters and gets down on her hands and knees to bark at her like a dog! I find it very upsetting to watch. It makes me realise that we're all so busy with our own lives that we don't always have time to stop and think about how some children are suffering.

---

* Now CoramBAAF.

Everyone is a little more familiar with each other today and there's a lot more in the way of debate. I'm particularly interested in learning more about parent–child attachment. Charlie and I have a very strong bond and I hope that I will have a similar bond with an adopted son or daughter. We talk about identity and how we need to preserve our adopted child's identity by not changing their first name; it is a gift from their birth parents. I think we all find this a difficult concept. If a child has been subjected to abuse in their family, then would their name not be linked to their trauma? The Indian couple in the group are particularly adamant that they'd like to change a child's name and they talk to the social workers privately afterwards. The group is told that if we can't accept this, then maybe we should reconsider whether adoption is right for us.

14 November 2013: Day 3
It is the final day of training and today's topics are adoptive parenting, therapeutic parenting, contact, and adoption support.

The contact element of today's course is going to be difficult for Dan. He hasn't wanted to have any contact with his birth family. He argues with the two social workers and in the end they tell us that if we can't change our attitudes towards contact, then maybe adoption isn't the right way forward for us. I'm most concerned by this and in the break we speak to the course leaders and explain Dan's situation. They say that they understand his perspective, but tell us that this is something we will have to work through in the next stage of the process.

We then move on to talk about therapeutic parenting and are told that being adoptive parents is different from being the parents of a birth child. As an example, we are asked if we would withhold food from a child. A few couples, including Dan and me, say that yes, we would. It is then explained that food is a big issue for lots of adopted children because they may never have had enough to eat. One couple explains that what they meant is that if a child asked for a Mars bar five minutes before a meal, they would refuse it until after the meal, not that they would withhold a main meal as a punishment.

It's been a long three days and we've met some lovely people, but it seems unlikely that we'll keep in touch with any of them as we all live in different areas. I think it's going to be difficult to go back to work tomorrow after the discussions we have had, but we've now completed Stage One of the adoption process!

4

The home assessment

December 2013–March 2014

Sunday 22 December 2013

The call came a couple of weeks ago to arrange the first meeting of Stage Two, the home assessment. The social worker who will take us through this part is called Lorraine; we've spoken on the telephone and she's asked if she can meet first with just Dan and me. We went to a Christmas concert last night so we'd already arranged for Charlie to have a sleepover at his Nana Jean's house. I'm quite nervous about today's meeting as Lorraine sounds authoritative, with a commanding voice on the telephone.

Lorraine arrives promptly and starts at once by booking in all of the next meetings and a panel date! Our local authority is linked with three others and Lorraine works for this consortium. This is the sort of "no nonsense, let's get things done" approach that Dan and I both appreciate and we warm to Lorraine immediately; she's down to earth, matter of fact, and we feel that she will soon get our measure.

'Right,' says Lorraine, 'I'll tell you about me because

I'm going to know everything about you except the inside of your cat's backside!' Dan and I are taken aback and start to laugh nervously. Lorraine tells us that she has adopted two of her children and also has birth children – we feel that we couldn't have a better person to guide us through Stage Two.

It's our turn now and Lorraine wants to know how we met and what attracted us to each other. The "how we met" is easy, but we both feel a bit embarrassed saying in front of each other what the attraction was! We answer the question but both of us are squirming.

We then try to describe our relationship. Lorraine is interested to learn how we resolve conflict and how we make joint decisions. It's another easy one for us because as we're similar in our approach to parenting, we don't tend to disagree when it comes to decisions about Charlie's upbringing. We don't argue either; we may get annoyed with each other at times, but rather than argue, we both walk away from the situation and have a discussion later, when the dust has settled.

Next, we talk about how we've prepared Charlie; he's only five and we have explained to him in a way that we think is appropriate for his age that some parents are unable to look after their children or keep them safe. Some time afterwards, Dan, Charlie and I were enjoying a walk in our neighbourhood when we noticed that Charlie was quietly crying.

'What's the matter, Charlie?'

'I'm just thinking about how sad it is that some children can't stay with their mummy or daddy.'

I tell Lorraine that I'm worried about how the whole adoption process is going to affect Charlie. I don't want him to be spoken to without either Dan or myself present and really want him to have as little involvement with social workers as possible.

Finally, we discuss the children whom we hope to

adopt. Since the training, Dan and I have had many discussions about the sex of an adopted child and have decided that we would prefer to adopt a girl. We want to limit sibling rivalry, and we think it would be greater between two boys. We also want to avoid possible comparisons between parenting an adopted little boy and our experiences with Charlie. Lorraine suggests that we apply to adopt a little girl aged 0–2 years because a pre-verbal child will be less disruptive for Charlie. We agree that this will be best in our circumstances.

Well, we have covered a lot of ground in the first three-hour meeting and I can't believe it, but I'm actually looking forward to the next one.

Sunday 29 December 2013
Christmas has been and gone. It's been lovely, and we've both been a bit over the top with presents for Charlie, as we're aware that it could be his last Christmas on his own.

Lorraine wants to see the three of us together this time to go over our family tree that we have prepared. She gets Charlie involved by asking him to fill in the gaps. Lorraine is lovely with him – she gets down on the floor and they talk about the members of our family and how often we see them. She has put to bed my fears for him; he seems quite relaxed with the whole situation. But soon, like any five-year-old boy, he gets bored and wants to play in his bedroom. Lorraine is happy with that and we then talk about our support network and who will complete our references. Officially, we need one family member and four friends, but Lorraine tells us that whenever possible she asks for both sets of the applicants' parents to be referees in order to avoid any family conflict. She will then visit both sets of parents and pick two friends to interview. We've already contacted our friends to check that they don't mind being involved, and they are all more than happy to help.

We are very fortunate that we live close to Dan's mum, Jean. She has to walk past our house to go to the local shops and often pops in to see us. Charlie has a great relationship with his nana; her house is a home from home, and even though we live close by, he still enjoys a sleepover. Jean loves spending time with her grandchildren and, like all nanas, showers them with treats and love. Because she has also been through the adoption process, albeit 40 years ago, she is a great support to Dan and me. Having someone close to us who knows how we're feeling is priceless and we're both so grateful for it.

Dan's brother, sister-in-law and niece also live close by. There's only a two-year age gap between their daughter, Amy, and Charlie, so they see each other regularly at school and have a close relationship. My sister lives about five miles away and has been a great help with Charlie, babysitting on occasion, and Charlie calls her Auntie Bonkers. When they're together, it's difficult to know who is the adult and who the five-year-old – it's good fun to watch. My parents live approximately twenty miles away and help where they can, but have busy lives themselves, with numerous hobbies, so we probably see them once a month. In all honesty, the main support network Dan and I have is each other. We know each other so well that we know instinctively when the other needs a break. We have plenty of friends who we socialised with regularly before we had Charlie, but now all of us are busy with young families and we catch up when we can with playdates or for special occasions. The closest of these friends have all agreed to provide references for us.

Lorraine notes all of this information and turns it into an "ecomap": we're in the centre and friends and family are in boxes around us with some text explaining how we are linked. Significant support is shown by a thick black connecting line, less significant support by a broken line.

Next time we will have our individual interviews. Dan's

is going to be first, on the following Thursday morning; mine will be on the same Thursday evening.

Thursday 2 January 2014
I'm at work when Dan has his interview. When I get home we don't have much time to talk as Dan is taking his mum to the theatre for the evening. He thinks it went well and says not to worry about mine. I am worried, though. I know it's necessary but I don't particularly relish the idea of picking over the bones of my past again. However, when Lorraine arrives this time, it feels like she's an old friend. She knows so much about me and Dan already, so I'm surprisingly happy to open up to her and give her the "warts and all" version of my early life.

We talk about my childhood both before and after my father left, and my feelings about it. I admit that I married my first husband entirely on the rebound, and that things should never have gone that far. But from this negative experience, I learned a lot about myself. I wanted to find an alternative to antidepressants to get me through this dark period. I found that meditation and exercise gave me the help that I needed and even today I exercise regularly and meditate if I feel life is getting on top of me.

After talking to Lorraine about this episode, I feel emotionally drained – it isn't a time to which I usually give much thought. I'm also concerned about the impact my story will have on the adoption process. But I've kind of thought to myself that I'm going to be honest, that I'm a good mum to Charlie and I'll be a good mum to a child we adopt: if that's not good enough, then so be it.

When Lorraine leaves a few hours later, I'm still emotional; it's been difficult recalling painful memories from many years ago and then explaining my feelings about them in the present day. The problem is, I can't be sure when I'll be asked about these times once more, so can't pack the memories away again just yet.

When Dan comes home, we talk about the interviews and Dan tells me about his. Dan told Lorraine that he found it very hard to deal with work pressure whilst grieving for his dad. He decided that he wanted to honour his dad and raise money for his father's favourite charity by running the London Marathon, which also gave him something to focus on and work towards. But the focus of their discussion was his own adoption and how he feels about contact. Dan has no desire to know his birth parents – he was very happy with his adoptive mum and dad and doesn't feel that meeting birth family members will add anything to his life. He is therefore struggling to understand why it is now considered in the best interest of the child to maintain some level of contact with birth parents and siblings. What is helpful for him is that Lorraine herself has adopted and her children are now teenagers. She can speak from experience about how staying in touch with their birth families has benefitted her children: they are not fantasising about an unknown parent.

Before our training I agreed with Dan, but we were advised to read a book called *Bubble Wrapped Children*, by Helen Oakwater. We had joined Adoption UK and I borrowed it from their lending library. The early chapters give great insight into the perspectives of the child and the birth mother, and I was able to see that some level of contact is a good thing and discussed this with Dan. Between Lorraine and me, we have been able to allay some of Dan's doubts and he is beginning to be more comfortable with the idea of contact.

Sunday 5 January 2014
This time, we are meeting Lorraine as a threesome again; she wants to talk to Charlie about the reality of having a sister. We've explained to him that it's likely that a younger sibling will get on his nerves at times, but generally what

Mum and Dad say goes in one ear and out the other – Charlie will take more notice if Lorraine speaks to him. She asks him what his favourite toys are – at the moment it's Lego, he's crazy about the stuff – and she tells him that a younger sister might accidentally knock down a tower that he's built or scribble on a picture that he's coloured. It must be very difficult for him to imagine at his tender age as he's only ever known the family unit being him and Dan and me.

Between meetings, we've been completing a chronology of significant life events, which we then go through with Lorraine. Reference forms have been sent to our friends and family for completion, and also to our employers. Fortunately, we both told our employers of our plans to adopt after we'd completed Stage One. Dan and I had decided that I would be the primary carer for our daughter and that I would take my full statutory entitlement of one year's adoption leave; time off and level of pay is the same for maternity and adoption. The company I work for is very supportive and understanding of working parents, and their policies reflect this.

We have also been asked to complete a financial statement for Lorraine to review – it asks for details of our income, the value of any assets we own, and the equity in our house. We will need to have life insurance policies, which are already in place; we don't need home or building insurance, which we find surprising. We also have to show all outgoings, not just mortgage and utilities but we also have to estimate the costs of childcare, haircuts, holidays, shopping and socialising. It's very detailed. Our statement seems to be OK, and Lorraine is happy to sign it off and doesn't think that we have anything to worry about financially. An adoption allowance can be claimed in some circumstances, but Lorraine says that we wouldn't qualify because our joint incomes are too high.

Monday 6 January 2014

The next meeting is the final one with Lorraine before our panel date, and it's a little sad because we've got used to her visits and they make us feel like we're moving ever closer to bringing a daughter home. Lorraine tells us that she's been in contact with the Head of Children's Services and that there is a little girl who would be a great match for us. However, there could be a family link to the area where I work, so there is going to be an internal risk assessment. Lorraine thinks that if this child is right for us, she could be home with us by the end of May! If the risk is considered too great, there are several little girls coming through the court system who could be a good match. It's a really strange feeling – I'm beyond excitement with the thought that we could be bringing home a daughter in a few short months. But the fact that there are several little girls who can't stay in their birth families and are living in foster care, and that we can only take one, is very upsetting.

This last meeting is a kind of "mop up" to spot any details that Lorraine thinks we've missed, but the main purpose is to discuss matching criteria: basically, to make a decision about the sex and age of the child we hope to adopt and what level of difficulty or disability, if any, we could cope with. We have to say whether we would consider a child who has been the victim of sexual abuse, domestic violence, substance misuse, non-accidental injury or a child who has learning difficulties, autism, Down's syndrome or other disabling conditions. This is the bit that Dan and I have both been dreading. Lorraine tells us to be honest; she points out that we are already a family unit, and for the adoption to succeed, we need to be upfront for Charlie as much as ourselves.

We both believe that we would be able to cope with a child who has experienced domestic violence, parental substance misuse, non-accidental injury and developmental delay; we say that we would be willing to discuss any of the other conditions listed. It's very difficult to make such decisions for the age group that we are hoping to adopt, as many conditions won't have surfaced before the age of two. Dan and I agree that, as with Charlie, if anything were to develop at a future date, we would deal with it as a family and adapt accordingly. We're adamant that once this little girl joins our family, she will be our daughter just as Charlie is our son.

We have to state our views regarding contact; Dan and I both feel that we would like a one-off supervised meeting with birth parents and that we would support indirect contact with birth parents, siblings and grandparents. Lorraine is confident that we will adhere to any contact agreements made, as she's been witness to Dan's journey towards accepting that contact is a necessary part of adoption.

Finally, Lorraine conducts a health and safety survey of the house, which goes well. Everything is in order. When we bought the house we completely renovated it, and as Charlie was still a toddler, made sure that all of the new fittings were toddler-friendly. We put in a new mantelpiece made of soft sandstone with bevelled edges and a gas fire with hidden controls – the gas fire was really only installed for decorative purposes, it's never used. We have fitted a handrail up the stairs and enclosed the open bannister. In fact, we have done everything highlighted by Mandy and Sharon during that first visit. Lorraine is happy that we've minimised any possible risk; as we don't use the fire and have made a cushioned surround to cover the hearth, Lorraine agrees that we don't need a fireguard. We will have to put up stairgates and buy an anti-slip mat for the bath, but these are minor items that can be sorted just before our little girl is placed. We have a fire safety check by the local fire brigade booked in for the following Wednesday, so that the number of smoke alarms and any risks not picked up by Lorraine can be further assessed.

That's it – we say goodbye to Lorraine. She's received the completed questionnaires from friends and family and has selected who she is going to visit.

Lorraine visits my parents first. They tell her that they support our decision to adopt, that we work as a team to parent Charlie and that we don't let him play one off against the other. It's only a short interview; we've been very frank with Lorraine and she is confident that our friends and family will back up the opinion that she's formed of us.

Next is Jean, Dan's mum. She's very interested to meet Lorraine because I've been telling her what we've covered in our meetings and she is looking forward to talking about how adoption has changed over the years. Lorraine wants to know how Jean thinks that Dan will cope with contact; Jean says that it has taken some time for Dan to accept the idea, but that we will support contact because we will ultimately do what is in the best interest of the child. Jean tells how she and I have a good relationship and can talk openly about anything; Lorraine is happy that Jean is as supportive to us as we have said.

Our good friends Matt and Jill are also interviewed. We are so grateful that they've agreed to meet with Lorraine; they have a beautiful twenty-week-old little girl whose precious twin sister was a stillbirth. They are overwhelmed with grief yet don't hesitate to help us by meeting Lorraine. Matt has known Dan since secondary school and the two men met Jill and me at around the same time. Lorraine is interested to learn how Matt thinks Dan would cope if his daughter wanted to trace her birth parents. Matt confirms what Jean has said about contact, and adds that even before Charlie was born, Dan and I talked about an adopted child becoming part of our family unit. Lorraine tells them that, so far, the interviews back up her own perception of us as individuals and as a couple.

Finally, Lorraine meets a friend whom Dan and I

house-shared with for two years. He has a good insight into how we operate as a couple and again confirms for Lorraine what we've talked about in our interviews. She tells us that she'll see us next to go through the Prospective Adopter's Report (PAR).

Tuesday 21 January 2014
Lorraine has completed the PAR and wants us to read through it. She tells us, 'I'll change any factual details, but my social worker opinion is my social worker opinion and is not for changing.'

Dan and I read it together in Lorraine's presence. It's an odd experience to tell your life story to a complete stranger and then to read an expert opinion on what you've experienced and how you present as a couple and a family unit. It's a pleasure and a relief to read the report. It's human nature to think about your faults and what you're not so good at, but Lorraine has highlighted our personal strengths of resilience and adaptability and has emphasised that we are experienced parents and that we've done a good job with Charlie. We are more than happy to sign the report on the dotted line!

The next time that we see Lorraine will be at the panel.

January–February 2014
It feels a little bit odd that it's the end of the home assessment already! It's happened so quickly, but Dan and I agree that this pace has suited us. Once we make a decision, we want to move forward as quickly as possible. I travel into work by public transport and have become friendly with another commuter, Stacy, one of the mums from Charlie's school. Her son is in the same year, and after speaking for a few weeks, she tells me that she and her husband adopted him a few years ago. I then tell her that we've just completed the home assessment and we compare notes. Hers was a long-drawn-out assessment

with social workers missing meetings or changing roles and took two years to complete – she's gobsmacked to learn that ours only took around two months, but says that she was happy with the lengthier process as it gave her time to digest what was happening. I can see that the fast speed wouldn't be for everyone, but as we have Charlie and we want to shield him from a drawn-out process, the faster Stage Two was better.

Monday 24 February 2014

The Prospective Adopter's Report (PAR) was given to the adoption panel several weeks ago to enable the panel members to have time to read all about us, and to prepare the questions that they will put to us.

I am ridiculously nervous when we arrive at the local authority's offices! Lorraine is already there in a small meeting room going through her notes. The Director of Children's Services and the Chair of the panel come to say hello and show us photos with information about panel members so that we know in advance who we will be meeting. We are handed a piece of paper containing five questions that the panel would like us to prepare answers to. They and Lorraine then join the panel to discuss whether we are suitable adoptive parents.

Dan and I are left alone in the small meeting room. We read and discuss the questions – they are pretty standard; why a girl, what can we offer, etc. We write our answers and decide that as I am going to be taking time off work to care for our daughter, I should be the one to address the panel.

We wait for what seems forever until the panel Chair comes to collect us. We follow her to a large boardroom and I can't believe how many people are in the room – there must be around twelve, not including me, Dan and Lorraine. The panel members take it in turn to introduce themselves – they are adoptive parents, a child psychologist and an elected council member, as well as social workers, and it's incredibly intimidating. The Chair of the panel asks each question and I answer, with Dan filling in any gaps whenever nerves get the better of me. In my working life I've attended meetings in boardrooms with a similar number of people, but this is different – each person on the panel knows every detail of our life and is making a judgement about us. Friends and family have kept telling me it's a formality, but when we are sitting in front of a room full of people deciding our fate, it doesn't feel like a foregone conclusion at all! At the end of question time, we are asked to leave the room while the panel comes to a decision. It only feels like a few minutes later when we are called back into the boardroom (we could decide whether to hear the outcome in the boardroom or just alone with the Chair), and the Chair tells us that the panel recommends our approval! I actually start to cry, which is totally out of character for me, but it means so much to us both.

Dan and I immediately phone our family and friends to let them know the fantastic news and go on to celebrate with lunch by the river.

5

Dealing with the fall-out

MARCH 2014–APRIL 2014

I have to say that the whole adoption process, and particularly the home assessment, has deeply affected me. Recalling events from my childhood, the poverty, the abandonment and the poor judgement in my subsequent relationships has brought feelings back to me that I had dealt with many years before. I feel I am a totally different person now from the one I was back then. For Dan to sit next to me and hear my life laid bare was also tough; nothing that we discussed was a surprise for him, but the level of detail ensured that any mystery left in our marriage has gone! I worry that he might see me differently now. This is ridiculous of course; Dan is a wonderful, loyal man who loves our family wholeheartedly. But talking about abandonment has brought to the fore the underlying and unfounded fear that this might happen to me again.

It's been a weird time, reading the Prospective Adopter's Report and seeing the journey of our lives, and our mistakes in black and white on the page. Really, I should feel pride at how far I've come on a personal level and what a brilliant job Dan and I have done with Charlie. I suppose I'm feeling vulnerable because once the home assessment is over, you're left to pick yourself up and carry on.

After the intensity of the last few months, ending with the euphoria of being accepted as prospective adopters at panel for a little girl aged between 0 and 2, it's been difficult to resist the temptation to rush out and buy a wardrobe full of pretty girl's clothes – common sense does prevail, however. We've only been approved, we are not talking about any children yet; clothes would be jumping the gun a little! We can, though, prepare her room. Dan and I both feel that it would be a good opportunity to involve Charlie in decorating his sister's room. He likes the idea of butterflies so we look online together and find some beautiful transfers that we can put on the wall to make the room a little more girly. This was once Charlie's nursery and has yellow wallpaper. We decide to paint the walls a dusky pink and Charlie and I put up the transfers together. It gives me a good opportunity to talk to him about his sister-to-be and his feelings. We also need to manage his expectations – we've no idea how long it's going to be before he finally does have a sister! Charlie seems to be taking everything in his stride, but he does tend to go a little quiet when we talk about mummies and daddies who are not able to look after their little children; not that they don't love them any more, but that perhaps they are ill or can't keep their children safe. The last thing we want to do is to frighten Charlie, but I have to give him some level of understanding about why there are children waiting to be adopted.

Her room is lovely; we pick co-ordinating butterfly bedding, pictures for the walls and Charlie is adamant that she would really like some heart-shaped bunting and a door hook that says "My Room". I feel myself filling up with emotion.

Because of the change in the adoption process, there have been a couple of documentaries on television about adoption. The first was called *15,000 kids and counting*. We watched it with some trepidation, but it proved to be helpful. In our training, we didn't hear too much about adoption from the perspective of birth parents and this was something that Dan and I highlighted in our feedback at the end of the course. The first episode was about social workers making the decision to remove children from birth families, who agreed to participate in the programme. Another two episodes follow a couple of children waiting for adopters to come forwards and the transition from foster home to adoptive parents. The timing of these programmes couldn't have come at a better time for us.

The second documentary was called *Wanted: a family of my own*, shown in four parts. It follows children and adopters from the beginning to the end of the adoption process. We are venturing into unknown territory, so it's encouraging to see the "happy ending" for both children and adopters. The majority of my work colleagues have watched it and we have some good discussions. I wonder what Dan and I talked about before adoption – it's all-consuming at the moment; we talk about it at home, at work and even on my journey to work with my friend who's already adopted.

Now that things are official, Dan and I decide to speak to Charlie's teacher at school to let her know what's going on. So far, Charlie has been his usual happy-go-lucky self and we don't want that to change. We ask his teacher to alert us if his behaviour alters and we agree that we'll do the same should anything alter at home. Charlie's teachers, Dan and I agree that it's vital for us to work together.

Mandy from our local authority has come to see us again. She's going to be our link worker – our point of contact for being matched with a child. Dan and I are pleased as she seems very balanced, sensible and bubbly. We're told that the little girl Lorraine mentioned during our home assessment does have family links in the area where I work, so she cannot be matched with us. This is very disappointing but not entirely a surprise. It's been two months since Lorraine mentioned her and I felt sure that there would have been some follow-up after the panel if she was meant to be with us. My mother-in-law and my friend have already warned us that from being approved at panel to being matched with a child took them both around two years, so I've mentally prepared myself for a long wait ahead.

Mandy doesn't give much away during her visit. She wants to talk to us about the child we are hoping to adopt; she has a matching proforma with her and we run through it so that she knows what we can offer. It's out of our hands now – we have to wait! However, we do know that if our local authority doesn't have a match for us after three months of being approved, we can then look at the national Adoption Register and at the family-finding websites as well as *Be My Parent** and *Children Who Wait*, both magazines featuring children waiting for adoption. Dan is frustrated and wonders why we can't do this straight away after being approved, so that children can be moved into loving homes more quickly and so that we can feel a bit more involved in finding our daughter. I do agree, but try to be the voice of reason and suggest that we just trust the process and wait it out. I also secretly dread looking at those little faces and having to choose between them.**

In the meantime, I've decided to use this time to arm myself with as much knowledge as I can. I've read books

---

* No longer in circulation.

** Many agencies do encourage their approved adopters to make initial links with children whom they see featured in magazines or online.

and essays about attachment, about a method called Theraplay, which supports therapeutic parenting – something we touched on in training – and about how drug and alcohol misuse in pregnancy affects the unborn child. I've also bought a book about introducing a sibling by adoption, but the books I've selected have all been a little like textbooks aimed at professionals and tend to look at worst case scenarios. We do have the benefit of experience in parenting, so we're under no illusion about how difficult it's going to be, but there are so many unknown factors to prepare for. Even the social workers don't know everything that has happened to these children, or the full family history of their parents.

6

Love at first sight

APRIL 2014–JULY 2014

Mandy called last week and asked if she could come to visit us on Wednesday 16 April. It's the Easter holidays and I've booked a week off work to spend with Charlie, and have organised lots of fun activities and days out for us. However, Dan's mum agrees to take Charlie to the cinema on that particular Wednesday so that he won't meet Mandy just yet.

Wednesday 16 April 2014
We're not sure what this meeting is going to involve today; we wonder if it's to discuss our matching criteria further. Last night Dan and I had a discussion about the age of child that, in a perfect world, we would love to adopt. Dan doesn't want to go back to the baby stage, he wants a walking and talking little girl who can communicate with us, but I disagree. After all the reading I've done over the last few weeks, I think that, as we have Charlie, we need to look at a younger age group. I'm worried that I won't attach as quickly to an older child. In the end we agree that

eight months old would be the perfect age for us – still a baby, but probably able to crawl and starting to develop her personality – more fun for Charlie.

Mandy arrives and gets straight to business; she has a profile she wants to talk to us about. Dan and I look at each other and try to conceal our beaming smiles! The child is eight months old – do we want to hear any more? I can't contain my excitement and start waffling on about our discussion the previous night. Too right we want to hear more!

Mandy tells us that her name is Jess-Alyn and that she was moved into foster care at birth; she is developing normally and has brown hair, blue eyes and a warm smile. Mandy then moves on to talk about Jess-Alyn's half-brothers and sisters and her birth mother; unfortunately her birth father is unknown. This takes up the rest of the meeting. My mind and heart are racing and it's difficult to concentrate. Dan and I sit holding hands on the sofa with daft grins on our faces; we both just want to hear more about Jess-Alyn, but Mandy goes on talking about her birth family. We try to focus our minds on extended family members, but for us, at the heart of this discussion, is an innocent eight-month-old baby girl.

Mandy asks if we want to try for a match with Jess-Alyn, and without a second thought Dan and I both reply 'Yes'.

We are then given the "profile": an A4 piece of paper with two photographs of a gorgeous baby and a brief description of her likes and dislikes. She has the most amazing blue eyes and the longest dark eyelashes that I've ever seen. I can see Dan starting to melt; we need to rein it in and not fall in love with this little girl just yet. Both her social worker and her foster carer need to be consulted before we can even dare to think that she could be coming home to us! Mandy will contact Jess-Alyn's social worker, Sonia, and let her know that we want to proceed. Sonia will read our Prospective Adopter's

Report and let Mandy know whether she agrees that we might be the right family. We're told that we aren't able to keep Jess-Alyn's profile because of data protection rules – this is a little disappointing. Mandy advises us to try to keep ourselves grounded – difficult as this may be. I don't think I'll ever be able to forget that little face and those amazing blue eyes.

When Mandy leaves, Dan and I can't contain ourselves: we're laughing, hugging each other and bouncing off the walls with happiness – so much for reining it in! We can't believe that after only seven weeks since being approved, we've seen a photo of our daughter-to-be. We know we shouldn't be thinking of her like this yet, but it's very, very difficult to keep our emotions in check. Mandy has promised to call us as soon as she hears anything, and I just know that the days are going to drag until she does.

Friday 25 April 2014
Mandy doesn't keep us waiting too long; she called a few days ago to tell us that Sonia would like to meet us. The meeting has been arranged for this afternoon and will involve Dan, me, Mandy, Sonia and another social worker – a family-finder called Penny. I'm really nervous and am desperate to make a good impression. The house is spotless; the bedroom that might be Jess-Alyn's is ready, even down to the cot being made up. All that's missing is the little girl herself. Dan thinks that I've gone a bit overboard making the bed up, but I want Sonia to see that we will cherish and look after this child.

Two o'clock comes round at last and Sonia is the first to arrive, followed by Mandy and Penny. I like Sonia immediately – she's friendly and down to earth. Penny is also very pleasant; she's recently moved jobs from a neighbouring authority. Sonia starts by questioning me about my depressive episode and asks how I coped and what mechanisms I have in place to avoid it happening again. She also wants to know about my experience of abandonment and poverty. Dan is asked again how he feels about indirect contact with family members. I didn't know what to expect at this meeting, but I suppose I thought it would be more about Jess-Alyn and what we could offer her as opposed to more delving into our pasts. Neither of us minds the questioning – Sonia has known Jess-Alyn since she was a couple of hours old, and obviously wants to make sure that we are the right family for her.

Finally Sonia does tell us a bit more about Jess-Alyn: she likes music and is a comic little character; there's a child in the foster home with her called Jonny – he's only a week older than Jess-Alyn and they love to play together. The foster carer, who is called Gwen and has twenty years' experience, absolutely adores Jess-Alyn, having fostered her from three hours old. I ask Sonia if we would be able to meet Jess-Alyn's birth mother, and she tells us that it would probably not be recommended, given that we live only twenty miles away. I'm surprised at how disappointed I feel about this; at the start of the process I was adamant that I wouldn't want to meet, but after the training and the books I've read, I can see that it would be a good thing for all concerned. We take the opportunity to question Sonia about Jess-Alyn's birth father and she confirms that her birth mother wouldn't reveal or possibly even doesn't know his identity. Dan and I feel how sad this is for Jess-Alyn and the social workers agree. We're asked if this causes us any concern, particularly in relation to any future health issues. Dan and I look at each other and shake our heads. Dan doesn't know anything about either of his birth parents so has no clue about any health predispositions. If we had a second birth child, we couldn't guarantee their health either, so this won't faze us. It will be difficult to talk with Jess-Alyn about her birth father, but we'll cross that bridge when we come to it and take full advantage of the authority's post-adoption service to help us.

Sonia then goes on a tour of the house; she's particularly interested in the room that might be Jess-Alyn's, of course. You can tell that she likes what she sees and that she can imagine Jess-Alyn sleeping in the cot.

When we're downstairs again, Penny asks how much leave I'm going to take from work. We'd already been advised that I would need to take the full year's entitlement and I've discussed this with my employer, who was in full support. Next, she asks about contact with birth family members and whether we would be happy to have letterbox contact with Jess-Alyn's birth mother and three half-siblings who are with adoptive parents. Penny particularly wants to know how Dan feels about this. It's true – Dan has changed his mind where contact is concerned. After the home assessment, he came to the conclusion that although he hasn't been curious about his birth family, he would want to support indirect contact for Jess-Alyn. With that, Penny and Sonia exchange a knowing look and Penny asks if we'd like to see some film footage.

Dan and I sit at our dining table and watch the little girl from the profile come to life. She is adorable and I can feel the tears coming. She's dressed in a little tutu and is crawling along and stopping every now and again to blow raspberries to the wooden floor beneath her. She is PERFECT for us; her sense of fun is similar to Charlie's – Mandy has got this spot on! It's weird: we are telling ourselves to pull back and remember not to get too attached while our hearts are ready to explode with the hope that we are watching our daughter-to-be. When the film has finished, Sonia asks if we'd like to proceed, and of course we say 'Yes'. Sonia tells us that she thinks we could be the right family for Jess-Alyn and that she'll gladly recommend us to go forward to a match. I feel like I have to pinch myself, this can't be right – it can't be happening this quickly, surely?

Sonia says that they will next meet with Jess-Alyn's

foster carer, Gwen, as she too needs to be happy with the potential match. She has loved and cared for Jess-Alyn since birth, so it's important that she's comfortable with her prospective adopters.

Wednesday 30 April 2014

Mandy called earlier in the week to let us know that the meeting between all of the social workers and Gwen is due to take place today. I'm like a cat on hot bricks at work, my mobile phone hasn't left my side and I keep glancing at it expectantly, willing it to ring. Mandy finally calls us later that evening and tells us the news we've been waiting for – it's a match! My mind instantly flashes back to the image of a beautiful little girl blowing raspberries to the floor – it's etched in my memory – and now Jess-Alyn is going to be our daughter. I run downstairs and tell Dan the amazing news – he's as excited as I am, we just can't believe that it's happening. Mandy tells us that we will be invited to the July panel and that we will be able to meet Gwen straight afterwards. Our heads are spinning. I grab a notepad and start to make a list of questions: what soothes Jess-Alyn if she's upset? Does she use a dummy? Does she sleep with toys in her cot? What are her favourite foods? Does anything scare her?

Dan and I decide that we want Charlie to be the first person to hear the good news. We're a solid threesome and we won't tell grandparents and friends until we're sure that Charlie is happy. We agree that we need to take a couple of days to get over the excitement and bring ourselves back down to earth before we talk to him. We don't want him to feel that he isn't enough for us; what we want is for him to experience the special bond – both rewarding and demanding – that comes from having a sibling.

Tuesday 10 June 2014

It's been over a month since our last visit from social

services and a lot has happened. We've been away for both Charlie's sixth and Dan's fortieth birthdays – we don't know what to expect when Jess-Alyn arrives but Mandy's advice is 'boring is best,' so we're trying to pack our remaining time as a threesome with trips away and nice memories for Charlie. Being able to tell him that he's going to have a baby sister was wonderful, although it was a shame that we didn't have a photo to show him.

'Can we buy her some hair bobbles? I want to plait her hair,' was his first question.

'We can buy them, but she's only a baby so she might not have much hair to plait at the moment.'

'Oh, OK. Well, when her hair grows down to her bottom like Rapunzel, can we dye it blonde and plait it?'

I just go with it because his response to the news is so positive and I don't have the heart to tell him that it'll be a very long time before her hair is that long and we certainly won't be dyeing it! We tell him what we know about Jess-Alyn and that she lives with another little boy called Jonny.

'Well, we must ask him to come and play,' Charlie tells us, in the most matter-of-fact way.

We're still holding fire on buying any clothes, but after buying box after box of hair slides, chosen by Charlie, we decide to buy a pushchair just to mark the occasion. We choose one with a seat that can turn to face you – Dan's idea, and a brilliant one too for encouraging attachment in the early days.

Both sets of grandparents and our siblings know the news now and are delighted for us and desperate to see what Jess-Alyn looks like. Jean says, 'Just think, your daughter and my granddaughter are out there in the world, being put to bed, having a bottle and oblivious to what's about to happen'. I'd been thinking like this since we first saw the video of Jess-Alyn and often imagined our daughter to be sound asleep in her cot, all snuggled up, not knowing that we're waiting to meet her.

Mandy arrives to tell us that our panel date is Wednesday 2 July at 9.45am and that we're meeting Gwen immediately afterwards at 11am. She tells us to think about any questions that we may have for Gwen, to take close-up A4 photos of our faces, and to get them laminated. They will be given to Gwen after the panel so that she can put them up around her house for Jess-Alyn to get used to what we look like. We're also asked to buy a photo album and to put in photos of the three of us and our house, and to record a message about each photo so that Jess-Alyn can recognise us, our home and our voices. Mandy then talks to us about Jess-Alyn's health: she has an innocent heart murmur and we are welcome to speak to the authority's medical adviser to find out more, but she can't guarantee that this would be before our July panel. (We subsequently found out that it is recommended that adopters have an appointment with the agency medical adviser during matching, to ensure they are told everything about the child's health.) We decide to speak to our own GP, as he will also be Jess-Alyn's doctor when she comes to live with us. No matter what he says, it won't deter us now; we will still want to go ahead, but we do want to be armed with all of the information.

Wednesday 11 June–Tuesday 1 July 2014
We decided that it would be nice for Charlie to give Jess-Alyn a gift when he does finally meet her, so we go to the Build a Bear workshop and Charlie chooses a lovely white dog with fluffy sparkly ears. We decide to add sound into the toy so that when Jess-Alyn presses a button, the dog will respond. We have to persuade Charlie that the theme from *Star Wars* probably isn't the best sound to choose, and we finally agree on 'Give me a hug'. Whenever I take Charlie shopping for Jess-Alyn, I end up buying him treats too. I'm acutely aware that we have to be very careful with

Charlie – I don't want him to resent Jess-Alyn. It's a real balancing act because we don't want to spoil him either; you just have to hope upon hope that you are making the right decisions!

We do all have great fun putting the photo album together. The first three photos are of each of us on our own: Charlie is cuddling the toy dog that he's going to give to Jess-Alyn when he meets her. The next photos are of the front of the house, Jess-Alyn's bedroom, our two cats and then two photos of the three of us together. We make a recording to introduce ourselves and to describe the photos. It's awful listening to your recorded voice, but we can see that this is a brilliant way for Jess-Alyn to get used to us before our first meeting.

Dan and I tell our respective employers our panel date and I estimate that I will probably be leaving on Friday 11 July. People at my work all want to hear everything they can about Jess-Alyn. Dan's going to take two weeks' paternity leave and his employer is letting him take the time off for the introductions on full pay – we'll have almost a month together. I don't think we've ever spent that long at home together before. We've asked for introductions to start before the six-week school holiday if possible. We would both feel awful if Charlie had to be left behind when we go to meet Jess-Alyn. It would also help me to get used to her when she finally comes to live with us. Dan and I could then have all day with her and help her to settle while Charlie has the distraction of school. In all honesty, we were disappointed that we weren't included in the June panel as the decision about the match was made in April, and June would have been perfect to help us with integrating the two children.

We continue as normally as possible for the remainder of June. It's my birthday and I spend it with my work colleagues on an away-day at an outward bound centre. I wasn't really looking forward to it but it is actually a good laugh and a fantastic stress-buster. We manage to speak to our doctor about Jess-Alyn's heart condition and he assures us that it isn't a defect and he isn't sure why it's been highlighted; it's very likely that by the time of the follow-up appointment it will have corrected itself and she will be discharged from any further testing.

Wednesday 2 July 2014
The day we've been waiting for has finally arrived; we've packed Charlie off to breakfast club at his school and are on our way to meet the panel. This time it's being held at a children's centre near the local authority offices. We pull into the car park and are met by Sonia, Penny and Mandy, who are very happy and chatty, and we all go to the waiting room and wait to be called in. It doesn't take long for us to be invited into the room, and it's nowhere near as daunting as before. We recognise the panel Chair and a few of the panel members and Dan and I feel more confident this time. The meeting follows the same procedure as before: we are again given written questions and asked to leave the room to consider our answers while Sonia, Penny and Mandy speak to the panel, putting forward their professional opinions about the proposed match.

When we come back into the room, the panel Chair asks us how we would integrate Jess-Alyn with Charlie, why we feel we would be good parents, and who our support network consists of. Again, as I am to be the primary carer, we've agreed that I'll lead the answers, with Dan chipping in. Not many nerves this time; I have no doubt that we can love and care for this little girl. We leave the panel to deliberate and are called back within minutes for the decision: a unanimous yes! And just like that, we're going to go from three to four!

We are both walking on air as we go back to the car and we call our families; it all feels a little bit surreal. We are now to meet with Gwen, Jess-Alyn's foster carer, at the authority's offices and fortunately arrive before her, so we get a bit of time to compose ourselves. After introductions, Sonia, Mandy, Gwen, Dan and I all sit in a meeting room, questions at the ready. Gwen is nothing like I expected her to be; she's probably in her late 50s or early 60s and is quite small and very chatty – she reminds me of my nan. After a few minutes together, I think reality hits Gwen and she starts to cry. She is very apologetic, but you can see that she loves Jess-Alyn and is going to miss her. I ask Gwen for a recent photograph to take home to show Charlie, but she hasn't brought one with her – I'm very disappointed! I thought it would be obvious that we'd want a photo; I'd hoped that at last I would be able to show Charlie what his sister looks like. We've handed over our A4 photos and the photo album we prepared for Jess-Alyn, and naturally assumed that we'd have a photo in return. I move on to general questions and information about Jess-Alyn's likes and dislikes, but to be honest, I feel a little deflated.

After the meeting with Gwen, Dan and I go for a meal to celebrate and finally decide to go clothes shopping for Jess-Alyn. We know that she's got dark hair and that we can buy clothes for a twelve to eighteen-month-old. It's lovely to look at all the clothes and know that in a few short weeks our daughter will be wearing them.

7

Getting ready for Baby

JULY 2014

Thursday 3 July 2014

I floated into work this morning with my head full of the matching panel and meeting Gwen. At my desk is a "Congratulations" balloon from my colleagues, and any chance of staying calm goes out of the window as I excitedly tell them what happened at the panel. Later that day, one of the directors emails me to congratulate us on behalf of the company and I'm presented with a bottle of champagne – my colleagues' best wishes are overwhelming. This is no good, I have to concentrate for a couple of weeks yet – it's going to be very difficult.

My line manager agrees that my last day at work will be Friday 11 July; I've booked the first two weeks as holiday because the panel's recommendation hasn't yet been confirmed by the agency decision-maker and we can't start adoption leave until it is. We have been assured that this will be a formality in our case, but the July panel was very, very busy and it looks as though the final sign-off for the match has been delayed due to the sheer volume of work. On a personal level, it's frustrating as without this final decision we can't move forward to introductions, and time is moving ever faster towards Jess-Alyn's first birthday. Looking at the bigger picture, it's great that so many children are going to find their new families; the timing is out of our control, so all we can do is express our feelings and be patient.

Dan and I had a chat with Charlie when he came back from school and told him that the men and women at panel had said that Jess-Alyn could come and live with us and that she's going to be his sister. He's very excited and asks if he can see a picture of her, which of course we don't have. We describe what she looks like and tell him not to worry, he'll be able to give her a hug very soon.

Sunday 6 July 2014

Dan's mum, Jean, has been itching to go shopping for little girls' clothes, so we're off out for the day. Dan and Charlie have gone to a classic car show and will have loads of fun together. Jean loves to shop and we come back with bags and bags of beautiful clothes for Jess-Alyn, along with some treats for Charlie. I have explained to him that he's had six years with us buying him clothes and toys, taking him on day trips and holidays and generally having fun, and that now Jess-Alyn might get presents when he doesn't. It's a difficult one for a six-year-old boy to comprehend, so I'm happy to bring him an inexpensive treat to avoid any tension and resentment before she comes home.

Friday 11 July

It's my last day at work, and I'm not sure how much work I'm going to do today as we've got hot snacks on order for mid-morning, a meal at lunchtime with my colleagues and then drinks after work! When I walk into the office my desk is pink: it has been decorated with "It's a girl!" banners and balloons and there is a desk full of presents! I'm speechless! I give everyone in the team a big hug and start to unwrap the gifts. Individually, they've all bought toys, clothes and photo albums for Jess-Alyn and some Lego for Charlie so that he doesn't feel left out. I'm lucky that I work with fantastic people; it turns out to be an emotional day. Mandy calls in the afternoon to check in and to tell me that there's still nothing from the decision-maker. She also asks if we can make a DVD over the weekend featuring the three of us and a walk around the house and garden. We can borrow a camcorder from her office. When I walk out of the door at 5.30pm it feels surreal – I'm leaving work to have a daughter.

Saturday 12 July–Sunday 13 July 2014
We've decided to have an overnight stay by the sea while we wait; a last trip as a threesome to spend quality family time with Charlie. On the way there, I look at the hotel confirmation and realise that I've booked the wrong date! I never ever make mistakes like that, but I'm not surprised because my head has been spinning for months. We get to the hotel and Dan explains the situation and they shuffle the booking around – phew, disaster averted!

It's a beautiful sunny weekend and the days are spent in simple pleasures: walking on the beach, rock-pooling and eating ice cream. Dan and I are glad to see Charlie enjoying himself. At the back of our minds we both worry how his sister's impending arrival is going to affect him; he appears unworried and his teacher has reassured us that there hasn't been any change in his behaviour at school. I think we're worrying unnecessarily for the time being.

Once home, our attentions turn to filming for the DVD. We decide to walk around the house and take it in turns to describe each room. Dan starts off with the living room, I do the kitchen and garden, and Charlie chats happily going up the stairs and showing off the bedrooms and bathroom. In the bathroom Charlie decides to tell Jess-Alyn all about his mouthwash for around five minutes, which makes me chuckle. I'm a little dubious whether Gwen will be able to play the film as it's a memory card for a laptop rather than a DVD, and she admitted herself that she's not the best at technology. I remember from the training all those months ago, a foster carer explaining how she played a family's DVD over and over again in the background to familiarise the baby with the new family, so I can see the importance of doing it.

Monday 14 July–Monday 21 July 2014
I get a phone call from Mandy to tell us where to return the camcorder and to let us know that we still haven't had formal approval for the match with Jess-Alyn. I took a gamble leaving work on Friday and I'm crossing my fingers and hoping that we get the decision in the next two weeks; if not and if I have to return to work for a few days before I can take adoption leave, then so be it!

Mandy calls again to tell us that she's watched the film and that it's just right and will be given to Gwen. There's still no news about confirming the match, and the personnel team from work are starting to press me for the matching certificate. It's also only a week away from Charlie's last day of term, so it looks as though our wish to start introductions and have Jess-Alyn move in while he's still at school is not going to happen. Dan and I are methodical and logical people who like order, so we are both feeling a little bit frustrated and helpless. Jess-Alyn's first birthday is fast approaching and we want to ensure that she celebrates it with us. We both find it increasingly frustrating that a quarter of Jess-Alyn's life has passed since we agreed to the match. We have a chat with Mandy about our concerns and she agrees that it would be a shame if Jess-Alyn misses her first birthday with us, but she'll try to make sure that we are at least able to spend the day with her. Dan's not happy at all, and surprisingly it's me with the voice of reason, telling Dan that it's out of our control, we've made our wishes known and we have to trust in the local authority.

It's the last day of Charlie's school term and we finally receive a call from the Head of Children's Services apologising for the delay. The decision has been approved and we are to have a Life Appreciation Day for Jess-Alyn next Tuesday morning, agree the introduction plan and then go straight into introductions that afternoon! Apparently a Life Appreciation Day is when we meet all of the important people in Jess-Alyn's life and hear whatever they can tell us about her. Well, we've already met Gwen, and we've been advised not to meet Jess-Alyn's birth mother, so the meeting should only take around an hour. It's been a stressful week, particularly for a couple of people who don't like to leave their fate in others' hands. But we now know that in four days we'll finally be meeting our daughter for the first time.

8

Introductions

22 JULY 2014–29 JULY 2014

Tuesday 22 July 2014: Day 1

We had some wonderful quality time with Charlie yesterday: the sun was shining so we spent the day in the garden playing all of his best games, which consisted mainly of face-painting me to look like a zombie, covering me in sand, pretending to throw spiders at me and ending in a party tea – Charlie's favourite!

Today feels weird, I can't quite comprehend that in a few hours we get to meet our daughter. Bizarrely, I'm fretting over what to wear and it takes me an age to decide on the outfit I wore in the film we made – I figure that if she's been watching it as often as we hope, it might help her to recognise me.

Dan and I drop Charlie off at Jean's house for the day. His cousin Amy is there today and this should act as a good distraction for him. We'd wanted him to be involved in introductions from the outset but were advised that Jess-Alyn needs to be comfortable with Dan and me before we introduce Charlie. He will become involved from day three onwards and we explain this to him. I thought that he'd be upset and disappointed, but he seems OK with it.

The first part of the morning is to be taken up with the Life Appreciation Day and the venue for this is the same as for the matching panel. When we arrive, Gwen, Penny and Mandy are already in the room and we have a good chat with Gwen about how Jess-Alyn is this morning. Gwen seems more composed and relaxed compared to our last meeting. I suppose that although she knew that Jess-Alyn would be moving on, she hadn't had much chance to get used to the idea when we met straight after the panel. The Adoption Service Manager, Rachel, arrives and runs through the Adoption Placement Plan; this tells us all about Jess-Alyn, her routine in the foster home and the personal items that will come with her. It also tells us that Gwen has always called her Jessie and rarely uses Jess-Alyn.

Penny then goes through the introduction plan for the next seven days. I quickly scan to the end to the 'Congratulations – Placement Day' heading, which is 29 July! It's as though Rachel has read my mind, and she says that this is the shortest introduction plan they've ever made. Because of Jessie's age and the fact that we are experienced parents, it has been decided that placement on day eight is the best way forward. There is a meeting halfway through the week to review whether this is still the best course of action or whether introductions need to be extended. After all that worry, Jessie will be home with us in time for her first birthday. Penny is talking, but it's as though I'm underwater and the sound is muffled; my head is too full with the excitement of meeting Jessie. Fortunately, Dan is taking it all in and he helps to tweak the plan so that it works for us all. As Jean is such a support to us, Rachel agrees that she can be included in the later stages of introductions; I know she'll be thrilled. The introduction plan is precise and any changes of more than half an hour have to be approved by Penny.

We decline the offer to stay in accommodation near the foster home for the week; we think it best for all of us if we sleep in our own beds each night. It's going to be an emotionally charged week as it is, without the added stress of sleep deprivation. I don't drive, so it's going to be a lot of driving for Dan but he agrees he'd rather that than stay in a hotel.

Rachel wishes us luck and tells us that we'll receive written copies of everything that we've discussed, as she can imagine that we're preoccupied with thoughts of meeting Jessie. She urges us to be honest about how things are going and to let them know if anything goes wrong. Gwen leaves to get Jessie ready for our first meeting, scheduled for 2.30pm – it's so close now.

How do I feel? It's like the feelings you have before a first date: butterflies in the stomach, nervous, nauseous. Will she like us? Will we bond? Dan is simply very excited.

When we pull up outside Gwen's house, we both pause for a minute before getting out of the car – it's a momentous day and I want to remember every detail. 'This is it, then,' Dan says, and we're out of the car and at Gwen's front door. Penny answers the door with a lovely big smile. 'Jess-Alyn's in the lounge, waiting for you'; we walk through the hall and it feels like the longest hall I've walked down in my life!

In the corner of the room, sitting on Gwen's knee, is Jessie. She's wearing a beautiful navy blue dress with white spots and looks just gorgeous. I immediately forget that I am a guest in Gwen's house and that Jessie is a virtual stranger to us and go straight up to her and say 'Hello!' It's like there is nothing and nobody else in the room except me, Dan and Jessie. Then she looks at us with those beautiful blue eyes and gives us the biggest smile – can it be possible? Does she recognise us? Neither I nor Dan cry, but we look at each other and can't stop smiling; when I look again at Jessie I feel pure joy.

Gwen has put a few toys around on the floor and sets Jessie down to play with them, so that Dan and I can join her. I look around the room and there is no mistaking that young children live here: the room is filled with playpens, toys, baby walkers, baby chairs and a huge fireguard – leaving little floor space. Behind the fireguard are the A4 photos of the three of us and in the playpen is our photo book, which Gwen tells us Jessie likes to look at. Jessie's favourite toy is a pink Minnie Mouse baby walker and Gwen puts her in it. Jessie is at our eye level now and we have a moment of lovely eye contact. Then Jessie puts her finger in my mouth. I'm not sure why she does this but I don't want to discourage any contact. Dan has allowed me to take the lead to begin with and has sat back watching us. He joins in now and Jessie puts her fingers in his mouth too – I must remember to ask Mandy what this means! Penny is observing the three of us and takes lots of photos. After about an hour she seems to be satisfied that Jessie is fine with us, and leaves.

Gwen's house is very warm and the fact that so many people are in the room makes it even warmer. There are two fans in the corner but they just move the hot air around and don't make the room any cooler. Gwen takes Jessie out of the walker and undresses her down to a babygro so that she's a bit more comfortable; Dan and I take turns in giving her a bottle of juice and she happily takes it from us. We can't leave her alone, we both hug and hold her but are careful not to overwhelm her; she seems happy and doesn't cry or show any distress. It's four o'clock now, time for Jessie's dinner and time for us to say goodbye for today.

Dan and I bounce out of Gwen's house and back to the car. We can't wait to get home and show the photos we now have to Charlie. When we get to Jean's house, my sister-in-law is in the garden with the children and they are finishing off strawberries and cream. We want Charlie to be the first to see the photos of his sister, so after a brief "hello" to everyone, we take him upstairs into the spare room. 'This is your sister, Charlie', I say as I show him the photos. He looks at each one in turn and says, 'Isn't she cute? Can I play outside now?' I'm not sure that this was quite the reaction I was expecting, but so far, so good! We go downstairs and show the photos to Jean, Claire and Amy and describe the two hours we spent with Jessie. It's very difficult to convey a feeling of absolute happiness, especially when you feel as though you are still in a dream.

Later that evening, Mandy calls to ask how we feel the afternoon went. We both believe that it went well, but we're not looking at it from a professional perspective. We tell Mandy about Jessie putting her fingers in our mouths and she tells us that this is a very good sign. Rachel, Mandy's manager, often tells them how a baby will be fascinated with eyes, nose and mouth, which is why A4 photos of faces work so well. Penny and Gwen have spoken with Mandy, and both said how well the first meeting went: our getting straight down on the floor and playing with Jessie helped her to feel relaxed with us.

Dan and I are both emotionally drained; we've been building up to today for so long and we've now finally met our little girl.

Wednesday 23 July 2014: Day 2
We've arranged for Charlie to stay with Jean again. It's a much longer visit with Jessie today – we have to be at Gwen's by 9.30am and will stay until 4pm. Charlie is looking forward to another day with his nana and they're both off to the cinema – it makes it a lot easier knowing that Charlie is doing what he enjoys. The sun is shining again today so we both know it's going to be extremely hot in Gwen's front room. When we arrive, Jessie is asleep. She usually wakes early, "plays hard" and takes a nap in the morning and then another in the afternoon. We take the opportunity to have a chat with Gwen; despite

being an experienced foster carer, it must be weird having strangers come into your house when you know that they will eventually take away the little girl who has been loved like a member of your own family. We find out that Gwen is a widow and that she and her husband fostered together for twenty years. They had birth children and their daughter Louise still lives at home and helps Gwen with the foster children, as she has some mobility issues now. Gwen has a lovely manner – she's so warm that you can't help but like her.

It is hot again and Dan notices that the windows are closed.

'Do you want me to open the windows for you, Gwen?'

'Well, that's OK, Dan, as long as you can shut them for me before you go. I can't reach them, you see.'

You can feel the two fans in the room circulating cooler air and it's a relief. Jessie wakes up and smiles at us when she comes into the room. Gwen changes her nappy on her lap – am I going to have to learn this technique? I used to put Charlie on a mat and changed him on the floor. Jessie's a wriggler – I'd be worried about dropping her or the contents of the nappy! Jonny is around today too; he's being adopted by family members shortly after Jessie is placed with us, so it's a busy time for Gwen – two moves in very quick succession. He's a happy little lad, very vocal, but it looks like Jessie is the boss. Jonny is happily sitting in his chair and Jessie climbs all over him. They both like to watch Baby TV and it is on constantly in the background. Dan and I follow the same pattern as yesterday: we get down on the floor and play with Jessie and her toys; she interacts with us very well and puts her fingers in our mouths again. There's lots of eye contact and Jessie lets us hold her and sits on our laps happily enough. Before we know it, it's 11am and time for our comfort break. When you first read the introduction plan and see scheduled breaks, it's easy to question why you would want them.

After all, you want to spend as much time as you can with your new daughter, right? Rest assured, these breaks are very much needed – you need them, the foster carer needs them and the child needs them too. Feelings are running so high that you need time to press the reset button on your emotions. It gives me and Dan a chance to talk over how we think things are going and we agree that Jessie seems to have taken to us already. I ask Dan if he's OK with me taking more of the lead for the moment and he's fine. I'm conscious that I must not monopolise her, but I want her to trust me as I will be responsible for her day-to-day care when Dan returns to work.

The plan for this afternoon is to go for a short walk around the block with Gwen and Jessie, but when we get back to Gwen's house Jessie is still fast asleep. Gwen has prepared a lunch of sandwiches and scones and we sit and eat together in the garden. We've brought our new pram with us, and Gwen is very excited about the model we've chosen, especially the matching parasol.

'Oooh, wait until I tell Louise! We saw a baby in this pram on our holidays and thought it was lovely, and now our Jessie's got one – can I take a photo to show Louise?' We wouldn't dream of saying no.

'I know it sounds weird, but it's funny that we were saying wouldn't it be nice if Jessie had this sort of pram and now she will have!'

Soon Jessie and Jonny wake up and it's time for their lunch. Gwen has prepared it and feeds the children. Louise is a nursery nurse and has told Gwen about the modern method of "baby-led" weaning, where finger food is put on the high chair tray. Gwen does this and gives the children sandwiches, but isn't sure about this new method; she prefers to blend the food and get them used to solids in that way.

'I won't have them choking on my watch,' she says.

It's probably the heat and the fact that Dan and I are

there, but Jessie doesn't seem too interested in her food and throws most of it on the floor. I shouldn't do it, I know, but I immediately think of Charlie at the same age and what he was eating; he had a good appetite and enjoyed trying new foods. Jessie only has two little teeth and Charlie had a mouthful by the age of one, so I'm sure once her teeth come through her eating will improve.

As soon as lunch is cleared away, we go back to the living room for more play time, cuddles and a bottle for Jessie; she is still drinking four bottles of Stage 1 formula a day. 'She loves her bottle, I'll leave you to wean her off it,' laughs Gwen.

I ask why she's still on Stage 1 formula and Gwen explains that the health visitor said there was no need to move her to the next stage; we're hoping to meet the health visitor during introductions and will ask her why this is.

At 2pm the doorbell rings and it's Sonia, Jessie's social worker. She wants to see how it's all going. Dan is sitting on the sofa and I'm standing and holding Jessie when she walks into the room.

'Oh my goodness, is it only day two? The way you two are together I thought it was more like day five.' I can feel myself beaming. I sit down with Jessie on my lap and we read a book together. "The Wheels on the Bus" is her favourite and she enjoys my terrible singing! Sonia has a chat with Gwen about Jessie generally and how she's been over the last couple of weeks and then comes over to me and Jessie.

'It's as though you're a mum with her baby, come to visit Gwen.'

This is lovely for me to hear, but I do wonder how Gwen feels; she has a good poker face.

'I'm happy,' Sonia says. 'I don't need to see any more today. Jessie's happy so I'm happy,' and she goes.

I'm rubbing Jessie's head while she's sitting on my lap, and Gwen says, 'She won't fall asleep on your lap, she never does.' We all sit and watch daytime TV with me still stroking Jessie's head.

'She's gone,' says Gwen. 'Well I never, she's gone to sleep on you, she's NEVER done that before; you've got the knack,' and she quickly grabs her camera and takes a photo.

It's the hottest day of the year and I can feel that my top is drenched from Jessie's body heat but I don't want to move a muscle, I don't want this moment to end. Not much chance of going for that walk now, but I can't wait to let Penny and Mandy know why we had to change the introduction plan. I was so worried that this little girl wouldn't like us but it's only day two, our first full day together, and she's sleeping soundly on my chest. It's as though she knows that I will take care of her. It's four o'clock and we have to leave and Jessie's still asleep. Gwen lets me take her up to her cot. I put her down and tiptoe out of the room backwards – I can't take my eyes off this beautiful little girl.

We quietly say goodbye to Gwen and start on the journey back home. On the way I call Mandy and tell her about our day. Mandy is delighted, and I'm thrilled that the plan is working out so right for us – early days I know, but my gut feeling is that everything will be just fine.

We collect Charlie and tell him that tomorrow he's going to be coming with us to meet his new sister; he can't wait to present her with the cuddly dog that he's got for her. I'm a little nervous again. It's great that Dan and I seem to be doing well but I need to make sure that Charlie is happy too – anxiety that the two children might not get on sets in, but I have to put these thoughts aside and wait and see what tomorrow brings.

Thursday 24 July 2014: Day 3
Back at Gwen's house at 9am, and this time Charlie is with us; it feels a little bit like our first meeting all over again.

What if Charlie is immediately jealous – after all, he's had us to himself for six years, who could blame him? We asked Mandy if we should bring some of Charlie's toys for him, as it's a long day for a six-year-old boy. Mandy says that Charlie needs to spend the time interacting with his sister and shouldn't really be distracted from that. I then worry that maybe Jessie will feel crowded. This is ridiculous, I'm worrying about everything!

Gwen is lovely with Charlie straight away, and gets him a drink of squash and a biscuit. He's won over immediately. He self-consciously edges himself over to Jessie and says hello to her; she instantly puts her fingers in his mouth, which makes him laugh, but like Dan and me on the first day, he isn't quite sure how to react. He takes the toy dog from behind his back and gives it to Jessie and she happily takes it from him.

Gwen says to Charlie, 'Jessie's got you a little pressie too,' and she hands him a small bear. Charlie grins from ear to ear. 'She loves me,' he says and I breathe out. I hadn't even realised that I'd been holding my breath.

It's another glorious day and we're going to the local park. Gwen walks along with us to the end of the road and then leaves us alone for two whole hours! It's nice to be outside in the fresh air as a family unit. There's a lot of pressure for introductions to go well and it's nice to be "normal" for a few hours. We decamp on to the grass and Charlie runs to the swings to play while I settle Jessie and try to persuade her to keep her sun hat on. It's still only 10am but the sun is hot already. We have the park to ourselves aside from a couple of dog walkers and we're mesmerised with Jessie and her reactions to things. She can't stop touching the grass and seems to like how it feels against her legs; we take her shoes off so that she can feel it on her feet. Charlie messes about putting Jessie's sun hat on and making her smile and they both pose for photos. I couldn't hope for anything better so early on. We go for a walk around the park with Jessie in the pushchair and she soon falls asleep. People nod to us and we must look just like an ordinary family in the park – not in the early stages of getting to know each other. Too quickly, the two hours are over and we go back to Gwen's house and leave Jessie to sleep.

Gwen has a large garden with a trampoline and Charlie rushes off to the bottom of the garden, Dan goes with him and I help Gwen prepare Jessie's lunch. Today she's having fish fingers and chips. When she wakes up, I put Jessie into her high chair and put the food on her tray; she eats a little bit but again throws a lot on the floor.

'It's OK, I'll top her up later,' says Gwen.

Jessie's routine is all over the place this week because of the sweltering heat. She takes a lot of diluted blackcurrant juice so is well hydrated, but like anyone on a hot day, she doesn't want to eat too much.

It's time for us to take a break and we're ready for one. It's hot and Gwen's living room feels a little claustrophobic with two babies, a six-year-old and three adults. We're expecting Mandy and the health visitor this afternoon so the body heat is going to increase! We go to the same café as yesterday and enjoy lunch together. It gives us a chance to see how Charlie is holding up. All he can talk about is Gwen's trampoline; even when we steer the conversation to Jessie he changes it back to the trampoline. I take this as a good sign – he doesn't seem fazed at the moment. The true test will be when she comes to our house.

Shortly after getting back to Gwen's, the health visitor arrives and does a development check; Jessie is crawling well and appears to be meeting all of her developmental milestones. Mandy arrives too and asks us all how things are going. Everyone from the agency is extremely pleased, so there won't be any changes to the introduction plan and Jessie will be coming to our house tomorrow as planned!

The visitors leave together and Louise, Gwen's daughter, comes home from work. She's just like Gwen, friendly and warm, and she says, 'When we saw the big photos, we both said that Jessie's got the same nose as her new mum.'

This has to be a bittersweet time for Gwen and Louise but they make us all feel so welcome in their home. I'm going to be doing bedtime routine with Jessie tonight. Charlie and Dan leave around teatime and take two large bags of Jessie's toys and photos of Gwen, Louise and Jonny with them ready for tomorrow's visit. Louise and I feed and bathe Jessie before getting her ready for bed.

'When you crack bath time, let me know how you did it. Jessie HATES bath time.'

Louise isn't wrong – Jessie screams the place down and doesn't like being dried either; my goodness, that cry is LOUD! Jessie has her milk on my lap again and I stroke her face and she falls asleep on me. It's wonderful to know that Jessie has never fallen asleep on anyone before. I put her to bed and meet up with Charlie and Dan and we have our tea in the local pub. It's another good chance to check that Charlie's OK and for him to express any worries or concerns; none so far. When I check on him in bed that night, my heart leaps into my mouth; he's clutching the toy bear Jessie has given him!

Friday 25 July 2014: Day 4
Dan and I wake at 6am and start to run around the house making sure that the place is clean and tidy. Sandwiches are made and I've even pushed the boat out and made a lemon drizzle cake for the occasion. I've blue-tacked the photos of Gwen, Louise and Jonny around the room at Jessie's crawling level and put out her toys so that they are the first thing that she sees when she comes in. Dan and I have boundless energy; we're running on adrenaline and I'm dreading the inevitable crash!

Dan, Charlie and I drive to Gwen's, ready for the 9am mid-way review meeting. Mandy runs it and it doesn't last very long. Essentially, it confirms that everyone involved is happy to continue. Shortly before the meeting Dan received a call from work; his manager is on annual leave and they have a tender worth several millions to cost by the end of the day. Dan has been working from home during introductions but he has to go to the office today – it's unavoidable. Dan raises this in the meeting. If he'd known the dates for introductions well in advance, he and his manager could have planned their workload, but we were only given one day's notice. We fully understand that this will be a problem. It doesn't go down well, but what can we do?

Jessie is allowed to come with us in our car today, and Mandy and Gwen follow behind. It's a lovely feeling to be bringing Jessie home, albeit only for a couple of hours. When we arrive, we show Jessie around the house, each room in turn; it's what we did on the day we brought Charlie home from hospital. When we get to Jessie's room, we put her inside her soon-to-be new bed and let her explore. We've been careful to replicate her cot at Gwen's, so it's very plain: no mobile, no toys, just a dummy and a pink and white crochet blanket that Gwen gave her when she brought her home from hospital.

We change the TV channel to Baby TV and leave it running in the background, as this is what Jessie's used to. She doesn't pay much attention to the toys that we've laid out, but instead crawls up and down the lounge; it's twice the size of Gwen's and she certainly enjoys making use of the space! She crawls from one end to the other and back again at record speed. Then she catches sight of the garden through the patio windows and presses her nose up against the glass and stares out. We just sit back and let her explore for half an hour. I had thought that she might be a little bit reserved in our house, but this isn't the case so far. Dan and I prepare lunch and we all sit together and eat. It all feels very forced and unnatural – I'm very conscious that we're being observed.

Then Dan leaves to go to the office for an hour to meet his deadline; he will be back in time to drive us back to Gwen's house. I'm left alone with Jessie, Charlie, Mandy and Gwen; it's difficult to be a hostess, to keep guests filled up with tea and cake and play with Jessie at the same time, but I do the best I can. It's the hardest day so far; although Jessie is in our own environment at last, we're not acting naturally at all. Dan, Charlie and I love the outdoors, walking in the park, and exploring new places; we even enjoy eating al fresco when the weather permits, so to crowd into the lounge and stay there on a lovely sunny day is alien to us.

It's a stressful couple of hours, and we have tears from Charlie at one point. One of Jessie's Christmas presents was a pink rocking horse and we've put this out for her to play with; Charlie takes an interest in it and it makes a loud neighing noise that terrifies Jessie. She screams hysterically, I comfort her and can see out of the corner of my eye that Charlie's face has dropped and his bottom lip is trembling. I instantly rush to him.

'Don't worry, Charlie, you didn't know it would make her cry,' and he bursts into tears himself.

'We're all going to do things that might make her cry until we get used to each other, please don't worry – you didn't do anything wrong.'

Next, Jessie crawls over to the fireplace; we have a padded hearth cover and she can't do any harm to herself. Every time I move her away, she goes back to it.

'You might need to think about getting a fireguard,' says Mandy, but I instantly put this to the back of my mind as we've already been assessed for health and safety and I'm sure that Jessie is simply exploring and will move on to something else soon enough.

Dan comes home and I'm really pleased to see him. I feel like it's been carnage this afternoon and as we've got to get back to Gwen's, the tidying up will have to wait until tonight. Poor Dan is upset that he missed out on this afternoon, but now he doesn't need to think about work until the end of his adoption leave in three weeks' time.

We get back to Gwen's house with Jessie in our car again, and I help Gwen prepare her dinner while Charlie and Dan play football in the local park. The heat hits us in Gwen's living room; the house has been locked up for most of the day so the room is "melting", as Gwen says. Jessie immediately starts to be miserable and whingey; she eats a little and I give her a bath to cool her down a bit. When I give her a bottle, she is so hot and clammy that she starts to scream; she's inconsolable and her crying makes her feel hotter and hotter. In the end I take her into the hall where it's cooler and she starts to calm down. Even though she's only a baby, the travelling and the new surroundings of our house must have felt strange to her – I wonder if she's a bit overwhelmed and over-tired. Finally she goes to sleep and I meet Charlie and Dan in the local pub for our tea, and we talk about how the day's gone. Charlie is happy, Dan and I are exhausted – we've done an eighty-mile journey today and I've still got the clearing up to do when we get home. We've got some more bags of Jessie's belongings to bring back and unpack, but at least tomorrow we bring Jessie home and have the day with just the four of us.

Saturday 26 July 2014: Day 5

We arrive at Gwen's at 9am and Jessie's ready and waiting for us. We dashed around the shops last night, making sure that we had all the same brands of dummy, bottles and food that Gwen has – we're sure to have forgotten something but at least we'll be in our own surroundings and can pop out to the local shops if we need to.

Jessie falls asleep in the car on the way home so we naughtily drive to Jean's house to surprise her and park outside. As Jessie is fast asleep we don't think that we will cause too much harm. Dan knocks on his mum's front door and tells her that Jessie is in the car if she wants to have a peep at her new granddaughter. I can see Jean starting to get emotional, but she manages to hold it together and gazes at Jessie through the car window. She's fighting back the tears. We need to go because Jessie is starting to stir, and we watch Jean walking back down her driveway.

'Do you think she's OK?' I ask Dan.

'Yeah, she'll probably have a cry when she gets into the house; she'll be wishing Dad could see her'. It's at times like this that Dan misses his dad. He didn't live to see his sons getting married and he hasn't had the chance to meet the grandchildren he would have doted on.

When we get home, I call Gwen to let her know that we've arrived safely, and we all play with Jessie in the lounge. We eat lunch together and then decide to go for a walk round the local area. As soon as we cross the road, who should we bump into but Jean on her way back from the local shops. We walk with Jean as far as her house and Jean insists on walking behind the pushchair so that Jessie doesn't see her.

It's a lovely relaxed day with lots of cuddling and eye contact, but as wonderful as our time together is, I'm clock-watching, conscious that we can't be late returning Jessie or deviate from the plan by more than half an hour. At 4pm we gather Jessie's things together and return to Gwen's. I carry Jessie into Gwen's lounge and try to hand her back but Jessie pulls away from Gwen and doesn't want me to let her go.

'Thanks very much, Jessie!' Gwen is joking but you can see in her face that she's hurt. When we finally say goodbye, Jessie cries for us and I feel like I want to sweep her up in my arms and take her home, but we've only got a couple of days left until she's home for good and we must be patient.

Charlie nods off in the car on the way home and Dan gently carries him to bed. He's been so well behaved and has played so nicely with Jessie, and we've praised him. Dan and I are absolutely exhausted: the heat, emotions and travelling are taking their toll so, as it's Saturday, we decide to watch a movie with a glass of wine and try to relax. At around 8pm we have a text from Mandy:

'How's it all gone today? Did you manage to get a fireguard?' I jump out of my chair: 'WHAT!' I thought the fireguard was an aside, something to think about if we feel it's necessary, so I reply:

'We've had a safety assessment by the fire brigade and we've been through the panel without needing a fireguard, so I didn't think it was a requirement, especially as the fireplace is decorative only. Can we have a chat about this in the morning?'

I can't relax now. Introductions take everything you have emotionally; we just don't have the capacity to think about finding and fitting a fireguard before Jessie comes home in two days. Trying to think about it sends me into a panic. It's 8pm now and we have to be at Gwen's at 9am Sunday morning; it's impossible. Dan wonders why this wasn't mentioned when Mandy visited and vows to call her in the morning. I spend the rest of the night looking online at fireguards; if we don't get one, does it mean that the placement will be delayed? I don't sleep well at all in spite of being exhausted – I'm going to suffer for this tomorrow!

Sunday 27 July 2014: Day 6

Mandy calls us while we're driving to Gwen's to discuss the fireguard; Dan questions why this hasn't been picked up before, especially as we've made all the changes to the house that we've been asked to do. We're also puzzled as we have already child-proofed the hearth. Mandy apologises and says that we should have phoned her last night rather than worry, as that's the last thing she wanted us to do. She says that this is something that has been missed and that she feels it's necessary for us to have a fireguard. I try to reason with her:

'Can't you trust our judgement that if we feel we need to get one, we will?' We can almost hear Mandy have a battle with herself about whether to let it go or not. She explains that she's maybe too risk averse and almost agrees that we can make our own decision on this one, but finally says:

'I'll have a chat with Rachel. If she decides that you need one, then you'll have to get one. If you're unhappy, there is a complaint form I can give to you if you want to make a complaint. I should have picked it up, it's my fault.'

I can't help but feel upset, Charlie is six years old and we have lived in our current house since he was younger than Jessie is now, and he hasn't come to any harm. I feel like it's a slur against our parenting skills, that by not having a fireguard we've put Charlie at risk – I'd agree if we'd ever lit the fire but it's never been used. We bought the fire and its surround with Charlie in the forefront of our minds and it feels like this isn't good enough.

Dan is getting really annoyed, so I try to be pragmatic.

'Look, if Rachel says we need a fireguard, then that's it. If we refuse, there's a good chance Jessie won't come home with us on Tuesday. I'm fed up about it too, but Mandy holds all the cards and arguing is pointless, so let's not waste our energy.' Dan very reluctantly agrees – he too doesn't want to delay Jessie's homecoming.

We've got on so well with Mandy during the whole adoption process that I've forgotten that, first and foremost, she is a social worker and that Jessie's welfare is her priority.

We arrive at Gwen's and stay for the usual half-hour chat. We get a lovely big smile from Jessie when she sees us, making the fireguard dispute feel irrelevant. We have a much longer day with Jessie today – we don't have to take her back until 6pm, and I will then be doing the bedtime routine at Gwen's.

We spend some time in our lounge, as this is where Jessie is beginning to feel at home. We sing nursery rhymes and play with toys; we've taken the rocking horse out of the room now – it's currently in the loft. Jessie doesn't seek out affection from us but she doesn't mind us holding and cuddling her. Charlie's great with her, which is such a relief. He's enjoying having both his mum and dad at home with him. Jessie loves playing in the garden with Charlie – they enjoy the bubble machine, sand table and generally being outside in the fresh air.

At nap time we put Jessie in her cot and try to get her used to it; she doesn't seem distressed and crawls around but she doesn't go to sleep. She nods off later when we're out on our afternoon walk.

Dan and I are walking on eggshells, trying to make sure that we're doing what Gwen would do. The photos of Gwen, Louise and Jonny are still at eye level for Jessie and she does crawl up to them and look at them, usually clutching her pink and white crochet blanket that she carries everywhere with her. After our tea we take Jessie back. It's been the best time so far – lovely to be together for a full day. I help Gwen with bath and bed and again meet Dan and Charlie in the local pub, where we have a snack, and return home absolutely tired out.

Monday 28 July 2014: Day 7
Today is our shortest day with Jessie and the last day of introductions. We're to bring her back to Gwen for 2.30pm so that they can have a goodbye tea together.

It's just Dan and me collecting her today. Charlie is with Jean, as this is the day when she will spend half an hour with Jessie – strictly no picking up or cuddling, but she will come and say hello. We collect Jessie and more bags of her belongings – we have five large black bags to unpack. I'm so pleased that we didn't go mad buying toys as Gwen has bought her so many – I'm not sure where we're going to keep them all!

We get home and Jessie seems to settle in straight away. Mandy calls and Dan speaks to her in the garden. I can see Dan pacing up and down and becoming quite animated! When he comes back in, he tells me that Rachel says we must have the fireguard in place two weeks after placement. We don't have a chance to discuss this as Jean and Charlie arrive. Jean says her "hello" to Jessie and you can see that she's full of emotion. She gets down on the floor and plays with her and Charlie, so we sit back and let her have this precious half hour with her grandchildren and take lots and lots of photos.

Once Jean leaves, I see I have a call on my phone from Mandy; she wants to see how we are after the decision about the fireguard. We have a good chat and clear the air. I explain that my concern was that the placement would be delayed and she is sorry that we thought that. We have two weeks to fit a fireguard and the authority will reimburse us – money was never the issue, but if we must have one and they are happy to pay for it, then so much the better. It wouldn't have been a big deal under normal circumstances, but we're not in normal circumstances, and it's easy to see how perspective can get lost.

Before long, we're back in the car again, taking Jessie back for the last time. Then we take Charlie to a nearby go-kart track for the rest of the afternoon. He's handled meeting his new sister, foster carers, social workers and health visitors brilliantly, and we want to give him a treat – it's also a chance to focus on him alone. It's all been about Jessie this week but he hasn't complained or shown any signs of attention-seeking behaviour. He absolutely loves his afternoon racing around the go-kart track, and although we've done nothing but eat out in restaurants for the last week, we have his favourite takeaway for tea.

When Charlie goes to bed, I decide that I'm going to make Gwen and Mandy a lemon drizzle cake each as a thank you for how well introductions have gone, so I stay up until quite late baking – it's a good distraction as there's no way that I'll sleep tonight. I can't believe that tomorrow we bring Jessie home for good!

9

Home at last

JULY 2014

Tuesday 29 July

Lemon drizzle cakes and flowers in hand, we arrive at Gwen's in excited anticipation. Mandy, our link worker, opens the door and the atmosphere is very different from the previous seven days; you can feel Gwen's sadness. She's been wonderfully warm and welcoming, always jolly and laughing, and the contrast today makes me realise how selfish I've been. I've only looked at today from our perspective; I haven't thought how Gwen must be feeling at all. Charlie stands in the hall talking to Mandy while Dan and I walk into the living room. Jessie is sitting on Gwen's lap and is wearing the same navy and white dress she wore on our very first visit. We quietly say our hellos and Jessie smiles in recognition.

My gifts feel ridiculous now – what was I expecting, gushing praise of my baking skills? I take the cakes and flowers to the kitchen and when I come back, Gwen is holding Jessie tight and says, 'You're going to have to take her from me, I can't…' and starts to cry. I walk over and take Jessie, who also starts to cry.

'Just love her for me, won't you? Please just love her!' she says and kisses Jessie goodbye, and with that I take Jessie and rush out of Gwen's house, leaving it for the last time.

'Don't worry, I'll stay with her and make sure she's OK,' says Mandy, and she sees us to the car, and we drive off.

Once we leave Gwen's road, I burst into uncontrollable tears.

'What's the matter, Mummy?' asks Charlie, and I honestly don't know. I've held it together for the last week but today has been too much. It's a mixture of feelings: I can't help but feel like I've kidnapped Jessie – I mean the way that I more or less ran out of the house with her and bundled her into the car, knowing that Gwen's heart was breaking. I'm overwhelmingly happy for us too; I turn and look at Jessie in the car seat and stroke her leg, then stroke Charlie's leg – she's coming to live with us at last, and our little family is complete. I'm feeling scared too, if I'm honest. Mandy and Gwen are at the end of the phone if we need them and we are to have weekly visits from the social workers, but this is it, we're on our own day and night from now on. Dan looks at me and he's worried. 'I'm OK,' I say. 'It was bound to hit me some time.'

We arrive home at last and settle Jessie in with her toys and put the Baby TV channel that she's used to on in the background. I call Gwen and let her know that we've got home and I'm pleased to hear that she sounds her bubbly self again. She thanks me for the flowers and cake and tells me that they enjoyed a piece after we'd gone.

'It seems a bit ridiculous,' I say. 'How can we ever say thank you for loving our daughter and for how great you've been over the last week?'

'Just love and look after Jessie for me, that's all I want for her.'

I call Mandy next and tell her how upset I was on the way home.

'I thought you were being tough! Don't worry, it went just as it was supposed to – it was a perfect handover.'

Mandy assures me that Gwen was fine once we'd gone; she stayed with her for a couple of hours just to make sure. Gwen knows that we will take good care of Jessie.

Phone calls done, I turn my attention to my two children playing together in the living room, and I can't quite believe that there won't be any rushing around later to take Jessie back. She's staying here for good! I feel anxious but more excited than anything else. Dan will be at home with us for the next two weeks, then I'll have two weeks of the holiday on my own with two children, but I'll worry about that when the time comes.

We decide that it's best to stay local and get Jessie more used to us and her new surroundings. The photos of Gwen, Louise and Jonny are still around the room and quite often she crawls over to them. We play in the house and the garden and take Jessie out in the pushchair in the afternoon where she falls asleep – so we just walk and walk until she wakes up. Jessie has eaten a little bit of her lunch and she eats all of her dinner, which is a great sign – Mandy warned us that Jessie's stress may manifest itself by her refusal of food or milk, but things seem OK at the moment.

All too soon, it's Jessie's bedtime and I tell Dan that I'll do the bath as I've done it before. I've put some toys in the bath and she seems quite content and lets me wash her quite happily – so far, so good. I bundle her into her towel and bring her into our bedroom and lie her down on our bed to dry her – and she screams and she screams and she screams! She does not like lying on her back at all, so I dry and dress her as fast as I can. When I pick her up to comfort her she hits out at me, smacking me in the face. Nothing that I do consoles her – she can't bear me touching her and keeps on hitting out at me. This is hard to take. I try to cuddle her, but this only serves to make things worse. Dan comes upstairs to see what the commotion is.

'She's really loud,' he says.

'I don't know what to do,' I say.

I decide to bring her downstairs and put Baby TV on, with Jessie sitting on my knee clutching her pink and white blanket and sucking her dummy. Finally, she starts to calm down. I'm shaken by what's happened; it's the fact that my touch doesn't console her that hurts the most, but why should it? She's only known us for a week, it's Gwen and Louise she's known all her life – we're strangers to her. Once she's stopped crying and is calm, I give her a bottle and put her in her cot. Again, she becomes very upset and begins to scream. I've tried to make Jessie's cot feel the same as at Gwen's house, and she has her blanket and dummy, but she just doesn't like it. Jonny had the cot next to her, so she's been used to sleeping in a room with another baby for comfort. I put a toy bear into the cot and wonder if this might distract her, but she turns away from it, screaming even louder – she doesn't like it at all. I take her out of the cot and she hits me in the face again. Dan comes into the room and takes her from me and she hits out at him too.

'I don't know what to do, Dan,' I say again.

I'm a parent – I've been through the baby stage and have a wonderful six-year-old son. When he was Jessie's age and upset like this, my presence in the room, my touch, my heartbeat, my smell, my voice soothed him. I'd simply pick him up and hold him close and he'd stop crying instantly – like magic. Not so with Jessie – nothing about me is familiar, all of the things that soothed Charlie seem to upset Jessie; bottom line is, I'm not Gwen.

'I'm going to take her for a walk,' I say to Dan. It's early evening and July, so it's quite warm still. I wrap her in a coat and blanket and put her into her pushchair so that she's facing me. Within ten minutes, Jessie's eyes start to close and very soon she's asleep. We continue to walk for another half hour until I'm sure that she's in a deep sleep before I return home. I needed the walk to calm myself as well, because I'm upset about the hitting out – where did that come from? Poor little girl, she must feel so confused right now, and as she can't speak, is she showing us her distress in other ways?

I gently carry her upstairs and lie her down in her cot and she finally seems to settle to sleep – PHEW!

'That was different to last week!' I say to Dan. When I did the bedtime routine with Gwen, it was precisely that: with Gwen and in Jessie's familiar surroundings. It's a shame that we didn't have an overnight stay built into the last stage of introductions, with maybe Gwen putting her to bed with me in our home. I wonder if that would have made the transition any easier for her.

Dan and I have a terrible night with Jessie: she wakes up every hour, and in the end I take a sleeping bag into her room and sleep on the floor so I can comfort her straight away. There's no specific reason for her waking up. What makes it hard is that it comes on the back of being already exhausted after introductions. Fortunately, Charlie isn't disturbed by Jessie – that boy can sleep through anything, thank goodness!

Wednesday 30 July 2014
I called Gwen this morning and told her about the night's antics, and she said, 'That sounds like our Jessie'. She tells us that this is quite usual; she doesn't sleep much at night and catches up in the day! We didn't know this before. We're all going to end up as sleep-deprived zombies at this rate – we don't have the luxury of daytime naps, as we've got Charlie to entertain too.

Dan and I are conscious that Jessie is dominating the living room: her toys and belongings are everywhere and she is monopolising the television as her Baby TV channel is constantly on in the background, as it was at Gwen's house. We decide to buy Charlie a television for his bedroom. I'd been set against him having one whenever the topic was raised in the past, but then Charlie enjoyed playing computer games in the lounge and watching his own television programmes. Because at the moment he isn't able to do this, we both feel that a TV in his room will give him a good bolthole if he feels like things are getting too much for him – all of this must be new and unsettling for him too. His friends have younger siblings, but of course they were inactive babies for most of their first year and this would have given the children a bit of time to get used to having them around the place. Charlie has been introduced to a crawling dynamo as a sister!

Charlie can't believe his luck. We explain why we are buying him a TV and that he will only be allowed to watch it for a set period of time. It gives us a chance to remind him that he can always talk to us about anything and not to bottle up his feelings.

Sunday 3 August 2014
The days and nights have all blended into one. I have absolutely no idea what day of the week it is. Jessie hasn't slept much at all during the night for much of the last week. We're just letting her sleep during the day when she needs to, but as much as possible in her cot, so she learns that this is a safe and cosy place to sleep at night. We have changed her milk to Stage 2 formula and this seems to have kick-started teething, so the poor little thing is getting new teeth as well as a new home and a new family. Suffice it to say, her pink and white crochet blanket is permanently clutched in her hands; it's the only familiar thing in her world at the moment. I've laminated the photo of Gwen, and when she's upset in her cot I give it to her and it does seem to bring some comfort.

Bath times are getting better now; she enjoys the bath

and plays with her toys happily, but she still doesn't like being dried afterwards, especially if she has to lie on her back. Dan suggests that we take her to the doctor: he suffers with polyps in his sinuses and feels pressure in them when he lies down, and wonders if this could be the case for Jessie. I wonder if she just feels vulnerable lying on her back, but follow Dan's suggestion and have made a doctor's appointment to have her checked over.

As Dan is still at home, we make the most of the time we have together and visit parks that we like a little further afield. We've been careful to make sure that we don't have any visitors and we've asked family and friends to be patient. We will introduce Jessie to them when we think she's ready. It feels a bit mean as our friends are very keen to meet her, but we have to get this right from the outset for Jessie, and the advice is that she needs to get used to the three of us first and foremost. However, on my early morning walk with Jessie today I stop at my brother-in-law's house so that my niece Amy can meet her new cousin. They've just returned from their holidays and probably weren't expecting a 9am knock on a Sunday morning. Jessie and I stay outside; we chat on the doorstep and introduce Jessie to Amy.

'She's been talking about Jessie while we've been on holiday,' says my sister-in-law, Claire. It's a shame that we can't invite Amy round to play like we did when Charlie was born, but we don't want to confuse Jessie.

It's another sunny day and we've arranged to go to the park and have asked our friends, Matt and Jill, to come along with their daughter Isabella, who is only a few weeks younger than Jessie. We've explained the "keep your distance" rule and they fully understand. The two little girls sit on a blanket and play together – it must be nice for Jessie to see another baby the same age as herself again. She really enjoys herself and loves the swings, and smiles when we push her.

At one point I need to change Jessie's nappy, so we take her into the large baby changing toilet in the park. As we know, Jessie doesn't like lying on her back to be changed and she screams extremely loudly until we've finished. Charlie puts his hands over his ears and starts to cry too, saying that the noise is too much for him. There have been a few instances lately when he has been sensitive to loud noises: he's been distressed at the sound of hand dryers and covered his ears and cried. I've decided that I'm going to ask the doctor to check his ears to see if there is a problem. I'm wondering if this is a result of Jessie coming home, so want to get to the bottom of it as soon as possible.

It's lovely to spend time with other people, and Charlie has fun playing football with Matt and Dan. We're sticking to no visits at our house for the time being and no visiting anyone else – just meeting on neutral ground for no more than an hour, and definitely no cuddling.

Tuesday 5 August 2014

Penny from social services is due today at 3.30pm and I'm thoroughly exhausted. Jessie is settling a little easier at night, but she is teething and niggly as a result. I've stopped taking her for a walk in her pushchair in the evening as I don't want her to form the habit. Dan and I put her in her cot and sit with her stroking her head until she falls asleep; this has been working for a couple of nights. She wakes probably four or five times in the night but settles again once she has her dummy and blanket, which she probably thinks she's lost during the night.

Dan takes Charlie out in the afternoons so that he can enjoy his dad's full attention. He takes his scooter to the local skate park and has a brilliant time.

Jessie has her afternoon nap at 2.30pm today, so I decide to have a little catnap myself before Penny's visit. I've got an hour before she's due, so should feel refreshed when she arrives and when Dan and Charlie come back from the park.

At 3pm I'm woken from my much-needed sleep by a knock at the door. I look out of Charlie's bedroom window and see Penny's car parked outside – she's half an hour early! I rush downstairs, not fully awake, but I don't want to miss an appointment. I'm worried it might look like I'm not coping.

'Hi there,' says Penny cheerfully. 'I'm a bit early, I hope you don't mind?'

'No, no it's fine, I was just having a rest while Jessie's asleep,' I reply, trying to catch sight of my reflection in the window. I bet I've got mascara smudged across my face and my hair's a mess; this is not the image I wanted to present.

Penny stays for an hour and we chat generally about how things are going. I tell her about Jessie not sleeping well at night yet and that she's teething. Penny is interested to know if Jessie is refusing food or milk, which she isn't. I tell her that we've registered her with our doctor and will be taking her to the next baby clinic to check her weight. Jessie is still fast asleep but I ask Penny if she'd like to see her; it's time for her to wake up anyway, so we creep into her bedroom and Jessie stirs – when she sees Penny she smiles and lets me pick her up and bring her downstairs for a little play.

Wednesday 6 August 2014
Dan and Charlie and I spent last night blowing up balloons, sticking birthday banners around the house and wrapping birthday presents. But we will be keeping it low key and won't be having a party or any visitors as we normally would to celebrate a birthday. On Sunday in the park, I asked Jill if she and Isabella would like to join us at a local farm for Jessie's birthday. It seems a shame not to mark the occasion with a day out – after all, we were so desperate to have her with us by today.

When Jessie wakes up, I carry her downstairs and we all sing "Happy Birthday". She immediately crawls over to her presents and starts trying to unwrap them – Charlie helps her and it's good to watch them. Of course, I take as many photos as I can! She has some lovely presents, but we're still getting to know her likes and dislikes, and she still plays with the toys she had in foster care.

We plan to have a full day at the farm and arrive shortly after it opens. Jessie enjoys looking at the animals and so does Isabella. Charlie has been to this farm several times before and likes to feed the animals and sit on the horses. There's also a tractor ride around the farmer's field that Charlie and I go on – it's so bumpy it makes us both laugh hysterically and I realise that I can't remember the last time Charlie and I laughed together like that.

There's a soft play area at the farm, which caters for children of all ages, so Charlie, Jessie and Isabella are all able to have fun. Jessie and Isabella sit in a soft play ball pool and have a good explore; they have it to themselves until an older girl joins them and starts to take the balls away from them. I have to laugh as Jessie crawls over to the girl and takes a ball back. 'That's my girl,' I think to myself.

It's interesting to see the different relationship that Jill and Isabella have, compared to me and Jessie. Isabella has only known Jill as her mum and obviously responds to Jill's voice and looks for her often while playing, but Jessie doesn't do this. I call her and she doesn't respond to me. She looks around as she recognises her name but smiles at anyone in the crowd who smiles at her; she doesn't recognise my voice. She's only lived with us for a week and I know I'm expecting too much too early, but that doesn't stop me from feeling sad.

When we get home, we have a birthday tea. I've made a white chocolate sponge with homemade strawberry jam decorated with butterflies – it's a bit of a hotchpotch as I'm so tired from broken sleep, but I was determined that I'd make Jessie's cake, just as I've made Charlie's every year.

Dan and I put Jessie to bed and stay with her until she's asleep, as we have done on previous nights. She's had a full day so doesn't fight sleep tonight.

'Please sleep well,' we both say as we leave her room – I'd forgotten how hard it is to function when you are sleep-deprived. This isn't being much fun for Charlie – this time last year we were in Paris having a wonderful family holiday, and this year he's visiting park after park with no holiday to look forward to.

'That's it, we're going to have a break,' Dan says. 'We've had a stressful month, let's get ourselves to Wales and get some sea air into our lungs; we could all do with it.'

I agree it's what we all need, but is now the right time?

10

Can we really do this?

AUGUST 2014–OCTOBER 2014

Thursday 7 August–Monday 25 August 2014
It's been very difficult to tell the difference between one day and the next; they have all blended into one. Dan and I have been on autopilot tending to Jessie and making sure that Charlie is coping.

We've taken Jessie to meet my mum and dad. We met on neutral ground at a park close to where they live and for no more than an hour. They were very excited to see her at last, and it was a shame that we couldn't stay with them for longer, but I'm very aware that we need to follow the advice to take introductions slowly. We have introduced all of our immediate family now. My sister Joanne popped round for half an hour to see Jessie and has promised Charlie that she'll take him out for the day. I'm really looking forward to her doing that; Charlie loves to spend time with her and it would help relieve some of the pressure.

I've let Dan talk me into booking a break for the four of us and we're going to Wales for a couple of nights on 5 and 6 September. It's back to a hotel we know, and as we are so well acquainted with the area, I'm confident that we will be able to entertain Jessie. I'm actually looking forward to walking on the beach and breathing in the sea air.

The weekly visits from the social workers are going well and they seem happy with how we're bonding. However, there has been some bad news regarding Jessie's social worker, Sonia: she called me to let me know that she's changing jobs and moving to a different authority. I'm concerned as Sonia knows Jessie's birth mother and has known Jessie for her whole life. When I tell Dan, he is worried how this will affect our application to court; a delay in replacing Sonia will have a knock-on effect, which I hadn't even considered! We've a review meeting planned for 26 August that Sonia will attend, so we can ask her then how this will impact on Jessie's adoption.

Monday 11 August 2014
The day that I've been dreading arrives at last – Dan's going back to work! We've been together constantly for most of the last four weeks and I know that I couldn't have got through this time without him. It's now going to be down to me to look after the needs of both children during the day. Charlie's still got two weeks of his school holiday left and it's going to be difficult to find something to entertain both a six-year-old-boy and one-year-old girl.

Dan leaves at 7am and should be coming back home at around 5pm; the two children and I wave him off, and for the first five minutes after he's gone I feel very nervous. 'Pull yourself together,' I tell myself, 'and carry on as normal!' We play in the garden for most of the time, and before we know it, Dan's arrived home again.

That first day has gone a lot better than I thought it would, and it's a relief!

Tuesday 26 August 2014
As Jessie has lived with us for four weeks now, and the local

authority still shares parental responsibility, we have to have what is called a Looked After Child (LAC) Review to check that everyone is happy with how the placement is going. Not only do all of the social workers involved with Jessie attend, but it's chaired by an Independent Reviewing Officer (IRO). It's been decided that the review will take place at our house as it's too soon to leave Jessie with anyone else, so at 2.30pm, on the dot, there is an influx of people: Sonia (Jessie's social worker), Mandy (our social worker), Penny (the family-finder) and Christine (the IRO). Charlie's still on holiday, so he'll be around too but will no doubt escape to his bedroom after the initial introductions. Dan and I made a mad dash to the shops this morning as we realised that we didn't have enough cups if everyone wanted a hot drink but – guess what – nobody wants one!

Charlie is a little extrovert and enjoys having an audience. He keeps the visitors entertained talking about Michael Jackson songs while I make cold drinks for everyone – fortunately we have enough glasses! Once we're all settled, I ask Charlie if he wouldn't mind watching TV in his room for a short while – he's a good lad and goes to his room without argument.

Weirdly, the Chair asks us all to introduce ourselves. I say weirdly, because it's our home and it feels strange to have a formal meeting held in this setting. After introductions the talk hardly involves us; it is more about what each social worker has done or still needs to do in relation to our case. In the end, I sit on the floor with Jessie and play with her to keep her happy; it doesn't seem that we will have any input today. However, after an hour we're asked how Jessie is and how her health has been. I say that I've registered her with the doctor and we've attended the baby clinic, and I produce her red medical book to show that her weight has increased. I mention that I've already taken Jessie to the GP to follow up Dan's hunch about her sinuses. She does in fact seem to have a similar condition to Dan's and the doctor gave me some saline drops and antihistamine that should help to ease it. He looked back at her medical records and saw that she was a "snuffly baby", and printed off a fact sheet for me. I'm a little concerned that this hasn't been mentioned and I can't help but wonder if there's anything else I don't know. Jessie's immunisations are scheduled for next week, and we've also joined the local children's centre and are hoping to start attending a music and nursery rhyme group from next Monday.

I raise our concern over Jessie's eating of solids, as she only wants bottles or blended food – any hint of lumps and she won't eat it at all. I've given up with sandwiches and finger food as they are thrown on the floor without even trying them – the same goes for any type of fruit. She cries when I try to give her a banana; I have to blend all fruit so that it's completely smooth. The social workers all agree that we shouldn't worry about it – the health visitors said the same when I mentioned it at baby clinic – but it doesn't seem right to me! (I've talked to people since, and realise that I could have asked to speak to the agency's medical adviser.) I'm worried that she might have regressed because of the move, but nobody else seems to pick up on it so maybe I'm over-thinking the situation. I'll just keep trying to encourage Jessie, and if there's no improvement in the next few weeks, I will mention it again.

The next LAC review meeting is set for Friday 7 November, and if all goes well we can then apply to court and legally adopt Jessie. Mandy suggests that the statutory visits reduce from weekly to fortnightly and the Chair agrees. I'm surprised and disappointed; I don't know why, but I'd assumed that we'd move to monthly meetings after today. I know that the visits are statutory, but for me they are a constant reminder that Jessie is not ours – they interfere with us fully bonding. I know that I'm holding back and feel that Jessie can sense this too. The adoption process so far has been intrusive, and so it should be. The children we adopt have been through so much that we need to be thoroughly vetted. But Dan and I have been approved by two panels and we're already parents. When I talk to Dan's mum, Jean, she can't understand why we're visited so often. She tells me how, after Dan and Ian were placed with them, she was left almost alone by social services, but had regular visits from health visitors, as was the way for all babies in the 1970s. I'm lucky that I can confide how I feel to Jean. She assures me that it'll take time, but that eventually I will bond with Jessie, and that the fortnightly visits will leave more time for us to behave as a normal family unit. We won't ever forget that Jessie is adopted, and obviously we talk about Gwen's photos with her and about her time in foster care, but we also want her to be treated as "one of the family", which is difficult when the visits remind us that she isn't yet, in the legal sense.

Everyone leaves except Mandy, who has decided to add an impromptu visit onto the end of the review. It's just after 3.30pm now and as Dan's taken the day off work, we'd hoped to have a couple of hours before dinner to spend together in the garden or taking a walk. Although the meeting didn't involve us much, I wanted to regroup the family and make sure that we are all feeling OK, especially Charlie. Outwardly he enjoyed talking to everyone, but I worry that a houseful of social workers might have some adverse effect: the spotlight was on Jessie again and he was sent to his bedroom, which I didn't enjoy having to do at all. Mandy stays for an hour and looks into Jessie's bedroom just before leaving – to check that it's clean, I suppose.

Dan and I rush around to prepare dinner for Charlie and Jessie, and I decide that I'm going to go on a bike ride to get my head straight after the meetings. I get my bike out of the garage and see Charlie rushing to put his trainers on.

'Where are you going, Charlie?' I ask.

'Out on my bike with you,' he replies.

'Not tonight, sweetheart. Let Mummy go on her own and we can go tomorrow.'

'NO, I WANT TO COME TODAY!' he says and I can see he's getting upset.

'It's a bit late for you to be out and the roads are quite busy, so let's go early tomorrow.'

'NO!' he shouts, and stamps upstairs, crying.

I wait outside the house and look up at Charlie's bedroom. He's staring at me from his window.

'I love you,' I mouth to him.

'I HATE YOU,' he shouts out of the window to me, 'I DON'T LOVE YOU ANY MORE!' and his face is scowling and full of anger. I've never seen him like this.

'OK, I'll go for a shorter ride tonight and you can come,' I say.

'NO, I HATE YOU!'

Dan's been tending to Jessie until now and he comes to the front door. 'What's going on?'

I explain, and he tells me to just go and he'll have a chat with Charlie when Jessie's in bed.

I ride faster and faster through country lanes, trying to cycle off the upset of the exchange between me and Charlie. Then I realise that I've got a puncture and will have to walk the final three miles home. It's probably a blessing in disguise as it will give Charlie and Dan time for a good chat.

I finally get home and, after showering, speak to Dan about this evening's incident. 'Charlie wants to talk to you,' Dan tells me, so I go to see him in his bedroom.

'I'm sorry I said that I don't love you any more, Mummy,' he says and throws his arms around me with such force that he almost knocks me over.

'Hey, come on, Charlie,' I say. 'I always love you, even when you don't love me.'

'Even when I say mean things?' he asks.

'Yes, even when you say mean things. But what I want to know is why you felt so cross with me. I've never seen you like that before; is there anything that's worrying you or that you want to tell me?'

He looks at me, and I know that he has something to say but can't or doesn't want to say it. 'You can tell me anything, Charlie, even if it's mean about me or Daddy or Jessie. You'll never be in trouble for telling me about what you feel inside.'

'Even if they're horrible feelings?'

'Yes, sweetheart; if you tell them to me or Daddy, then we can talk about them.'

We're sitting on Charlie's bed by now and he hugs me tight. 'It's about Jessie...I don't like her being my sister.' He blurts it out and starts to cry.

'Hey, come on now, don't cry. What is it you don't like about her?' I ask.

'She's loud when she cries and it hurts my ears.'

'Well, she's a baby and all babies cry this loud, but she won't be a baby forever,' I say. 'Is that the only thing that you don't like about Jessie or is there something else – I promise that you won't be in trouble.'

'I don't see you or Daddy much, you're always with Jessie,' he finally says.

'Well, Jessie is part of our family now and she's not going anywhere, she's here forever. You are right though – Daddy and I haven't spent much time with you without Jessie. I'll get Daddy to come upstairs and we'll all talk about what we can change, is that OK?'

'Yes, Mummy,' and I can see he's relieved to get his feelings out into the open.

I brief Dan and he joins us in Charlie's room. 'Charlie tells me that he doesn't feel like we spend much time with him since Jessie came to live with us, so I thought we could all have a chat about it,' I say.

'What would you like to do, Charlie?' Dan asks.

'Well, I miss going swimming with Daddy on Sundays.'

'OK, well I can take you swimming again,' says Dan. 'We'll go from this week.'

'I haven't been to the cinema with Mummy this holiday,' Charlie says, and he's right, we both love our cinema trips and haven't been during these holidays.

'Well, if Daddy agrees, we can go on a Saturday. We can have a look at what's on and pick a movie to watch this week. I'm so sorry that you felt upset – it's my fault and Daddy's. We should have noticed you were feeling like that. I know this six-week holiday is boring and rubbish for you, but it won't go on being like this, I promise.'

'Thank you, Mummy,' he says, and Dan and I both reassure him that he's done the right thing in telling us how he feels and to talk to us if he ever feels upset again.

And just like that, he's back to being his happy-go-lucky self.

Charlie is absolutely right: Dan and I took our eyes off the ball because we were so focused on how Jessie was settling in and coping, and didn't notice the pressure building. We're also sleep-deprived and trying to manage social workers, health visitors and introducing family members. All I can think is that we should have pushed harder for placement before the six-week school holidays.

Wednesday 27 August 2014

Dan and I woke this morning with what can best be described as an "argument hangover". After yesterday, I'm very worried about how Charlie is going to interact with Jessie and I'm expecting the worst.

Dan leaves for work at 7am as usual, leaving Jessie, Charlie and me together. I go into the kitchen and start to prepare our breakfast and can hear the children playing together. I should have known better than to worry – Charlie doesn't have a mean bone in his body and is being his usual funny and caring self with his little sister. I can hear him start to spin some of her toys and shout 'Wheeeeeeee!' and I hear Jessie laughing. I run into the room quickly and watch; it occurs to me that I've never heard Jessie laugh before. It's wonderful and I'm grinning from ear to ear myself as I watch them. They continue to play like this for half an hour with Jessie's laughter getting louder and louder. I manage to film them so that I can show Dan that night; I feel it's a breakthrough.

Sunday 31 August 2014

That beautiful laugh was the boost that Dan and I both needed, but me especially. Jessie's homecoming has been a shock to the system. Dan and I had heard all about how trauma affects older children and thought that we'd bypass this by adopting a baby – how misguided we were. Poor Jessie was taken from her birth mother as soon as she was born to live with Gwen, and after a year she had to leave Gwen to live with us. In a way, I'm pleased that she hasn't taken to us straight away – that she's making us earn her trust and love. We were naïve to think that it would be an easy transition for her.

It takes a while to get used to having another person in the house, particularly a one-year-old who has had such a huge upheaval. We've followed Gwen's routine with Jessie, but I'm not sure that it gives her any comfort, as her surroundings and the people in her life bear no resemblance to her first year of experience.

Bath times over the last four weeks have been a trial. The bath itself is great – Jessie loves the water now, but still hates getting dried afterwards; her cry is so, so loud and she's still hitting out at me to show just how upset she is. I've tried everything that I can think of to make it less unpleasant for her. I've warmed the towel to make sure that it's nice and fluffy (just in case it's the texture or temperature of the towel that she doesn't like); I've tried to dry her in all number of positions to see if it's lying down that causes the upset – but to no avail. In the end, I try a technique that I used with Charlie. He suffered terribly with colic in his first three months, so I attended a baby massage class to help ease it for him. I wasn't sure that it was going to work with Jessie, because I wonder if it's simply the fact that it's me bathing her that she doesn't like; she just doesn't trust me enough yet, I have to prove myself to her. The first time I try the massage, I make sure to warm the baby lotion in my hands before rubbing her tummy and arms and singing, 'It's time to rub, rub, rub, rub the baby'. I made up all kinds of songs with Charlie and this was the one that I used to sing when I massaged him. The first time is a moderate success: Jessie stops crying while I rub her tummy and arms, and smiles briefly – YES! I've done this every night as part of the bedtime routine since, and she doesn't get as upset when I dry her. I'm not going to say it's been a miracle cure – it hasn't stopped the crying completely but she's certainly not as distressed and doesn't try to hit me.

I've got it into my head that I need to show Jessie that she can trust me and I try to remember all I've read about attachment and draw on my experience with Charlie to build a bond with Jessie.

I try all sorts of methods: whenever we pass a mirror, I stop and point at myself: 'Mummy,' and at 'Jessie'; she doesn't say the words but she does join in with the pointing. She likes this and always smiles at her own reflection, as most babies of this age do, I suppose.

Charlie and I love to listen to music and dance, and quite by accident I found that Jessie enjoys this too. Charlie had asked me to play some music and Jessie was crying so I picked her up and started to dance with her, turning her upside down and spinning around with her in my arms – she loved it and started to smile and laugh and didn't want me to put her down.

It's been hard to juggle everyone and to take care of their emotions and my own. I constantly reassure Charlie that I love him, and that I'm proud of how he's getting used to having a sister. He still cries and covers his ears when Jessie cries but we've got an appointment at the hospital to check this out; I'll be pleased when we can get to the bottom of that one. I'm also starting to see that Charlie mimics Jessie's behaviour and I know it's to get my attention. I explain to him that being naughty is going to get him some attention, but not the sort that he wants; it's a lot to expect him to fully understand. He's a little boy and Dan and I are the adults, and we need to make sure that Charlie's needs as well as Jessie's needs are met and that we keep our promises to Charlie. So, as promised, I have a day with Charlie each weekend while Dan spends the day with Jessie. As Dan is back at work now, it's good for them to have some father/daughter time. Charlie loves having my undivided attention and after his outpouring, he knows that he is able to be honest about his feelings.

Friday 5 September–Sunday 7 September 2014
Charlie's had his first week back at school. I think he's glad to get back to his friends and he likes his new teacher.

I'm going to be a "school-run" mum for the whole of Charlie's school year and I'm looking forward to picking him up at 3.30pm every day. But I dread the first day, and feel self-conscious because I wasn't pregnant six weeks earlier when I collected Charlie and am now going to be walking into school with a brand new pushchair containing a one-year-old. The school playground is nowhere near as bad as I thought it was going to be. A couple of mums who knew that we were adopting come and say hello to me and Jessie and ask us how she's settling in. It's nice, actually – they don't ask any intrusive questions, which I think is what I dreaded. I worked full-time before Jessie came home so was rarely at the school gates anyway, so the majority of mums and dads wouldn't have known if I had been pregnant or not. I'm finding it quite hard to get into the routine of getting us all up, dressed and out of the door, particularly as I'm so sleep-deprived. The sleeping at night hasn't improved – I'm still getting up three or four times to give Jessie her dummy.

Against my better judgement, we are off to Wales today. We have joint parental responsibility for Jessie with the local authority, so I have to inform them of where we're going and for how long. There's a whole list of do's and don'ts that we've been given: we have to inform them of any accidents or bruises; we can't pierce her ears (not that we would anyway); we can't take her out of the country; and we have to ask permission for any holidays in the UK longer than two nights. I decide to tell Mandy about the holiday anyway, even though we're only going away for two nights. We don't need permission, but we are asked to provide the contact details for the hotel in which we'll be staying.

Dan has a half-day off work so that we can get the car packed and be ready to collect Charlie from school and head straight to Wales. We decide that we'll play it by ear and make as many stops as we need. Jessie seems fine with the journey until the last hour. We make a detour to a village that we know and stop to feed her and change her nappy. We also know that there's a really good fish and chip shop here, so Dan gives Jessie her bottle while Charlie and I go and fetch us a "chippy tea". We take it in turns to eat as Jessie is crying loudly and one of us has to hold her. She's been changed and has had her bottle, but by now it's nearly 7pm and at home she would have been in bed for the last hour. I've just about settled Jessie into a routine and I'm worried that the next two days are going to undo all of my efforts – Dan says we need a break and Jessie will enjoy it, but I remain unconvinced!

We finally arrive at our hotel at around 9pm and as it's

dark already, we decide to have an early night and to get up early the next morning to enjoy a full day of activities. The accommodation is a large family room with a second bedroom and a bunk-bed for Charlie. Jessie has a travel cot in our room and doesn't want to sleep in it. We try everything to soothe her but she's overtired and teething. 'Go and sleep in Charlie's room – there's no use in us both being tired tomorrow,' Dan says, and I don't need telling twice. I sleep in the bottom bunk and it's the best sleep I've had in a long time!

Charlie is very excited to wake up and find me in the bottom bunk and as Dan and Jessie are still asleep, I suggest that we have a walk on the beach, just the two of us.

It's only 6am but we're both wide awake and refreshed. The beach is a five-minute walk from the hotel, so we rush to the seafront to find that the sea is out and that we can walk along the beach. We have it all to ourselves – we run up and down, write our names in the sand and look in the rock pools. Maybe Dan was right after all: Charlie's relaxed and is enjoying the seaside; I've had a great night's sleep and can feel that my shoulders are starting to relax – they've been in the region of my ears for the last month – sea air is indeed the best tonic!

We need to be patient with Charlie. He's a kind and loving little boy – he just needs to get it all straight in his head. I told our social worker about the episode after the LAC review and she assured me that she'd have been more worried if an incident like that hadn't happened. 'Things will settle, but it might happen again in a month or two; it's normal. You're instinctive parents, so I'm confident that you'll be able to work it out with Charlie. If you do need help, please ring me.' I am reassured by Mandy's words.

Breakfast in the hotel is at 8am so Charlie and I get back half an hour before to help Dan get Jessie ready. Historically, family meals out haven't gone well; we took

Jessie to a café that we like during her first month with us and she became very agitated – by this, I mean that she threw the food on the floor and screamed – loudly. We've tried a couple of times since then and have had the same reaction, so have avoided more meals in public so far.

We order our breakfast and it takes an hour for it to be served; it's freshly cooked to order and the hotel is full. We manage to keep Jessie and Charlie entertained until the food arrives and although Jessie doesn't eat much, she doesn't get upset. I finish first and take her back to our room and get her ready for the day ahead. The sun is shining so we're going to spend the day on the beach.

All of a sudden Jessie's cheeks become red and her temperature rises a little, so we realise that she must have another new tooth starting to come through. We rush to the pharmacy and buy some supplies to help ease the pain. She cries but eventually falls asleep when the medicine kicks in.

While Jessie sleeps in the pushchair, we walk along the promenade and get our bearings. It's only a few weeks since we were last here but so much has changed in our family since then that the last trip feels like a lifetime ago.

The sun is beating down on us as we walk; we couldn't have picked a better weekend for our break. When Jessie wakes up, we decide to play on the beach; it's her first time by the sea. I strip her down to her nappy and after lathering her with suncream, sit her on the sand in front of me. She's fascinated by the sand and how it feels, so I cover her legs and watch her wipe it off. She thinks it's funny, and covers her legs with the sand herself and wipes it off, again and again and again. After the month we've had, it's nice to be still and feel the heat of the sun on my skin while listening to Jessie playing happily. Dan and Charlie are playing football further down the beach and when Dan catches sight of Jessie enjoying herself, he comes over to us and takes yet more photos. I want to record all of Jessie's "firsts" with us. After around an hour, Dan and I swap so that I can explore with Charlie; we paddle in the sea, look for crabs and find a dead jellyfish washed ashore, which fascinates Charlie.

By late afternoon, Jessie's cheeks start to redden again and she begins to whinge, so we decide to go for a drive around the local area. We've given her some more medication, and the car ride soothes her and she sleeps. Dan parks the car so that we're facing the sea; the tide is in so we enjoy watching the ebb and flow of the waves – all very relaxing!

We return to the hotel and try to lift Jessie out of the car without waking her, but unfortunately this doesn't work and she's very upset about being woken up. It's distressing to watch her – she works herself up into such a frenzy that she's inconsolable. I try to cuddle her but she pushes me away or hits me. I put her in the travel cot with her blanket and dummy, but she turns away from me. Dan tries to soothe her, but she reacts in the same way. We have to simply let her cry it out – she's been fed and watered, her nappy is fresh, we've given her more medication for teething pain, so there's very little else we can do except sit next to the travel cot so that she's not alone. The new experiences of the day must have over-stimulated her; she's had so many new things thrown at her that it must be difficult for her to process them all. Screaming is the only way she has to tell us that it's too much.

When we wake up the next day, we decide to have our breakfast and leave. We've had a terrible night with Jessie waking continuously, and we all just want to get home.

Dan decides to try a different, quicker route but when we reach the motorway we find long delays and we're at a virtual standstill due to road works. What should have been a journey of a couple of hours takes us five, and for the last hour Dan and I stare ahead in stony-faced silence while Jessie screams and screams and screams. I made the mistake of sitting in the front and try to distract her, but she's just not interested. Poor Charlie is sitting next to her and he starts to hold his ears and cry too. 'It hurts my ears, it hurts my ears!' There's nowhere for us to pull over and swap seats. I want at least to comfort Jessie and stop the noise that's causing Charlie such distress. I could quite easily burst into tears myself – there have been some lovely moments but this break has been a disaster. We shouldn't have gone away so early on in the placement.

I've never been so pleased to see my front door; my nerves are in shreds from the hour of crying that we've just endured. It's bottle and bed for Jessie and she goes to sleep almost instantly. I then have a chance to attend to Charlie and make sure that he's OK before he goes to sleep. The fact that Jessie isn't comforted by any of us is taking its toll – it's almost as though she's independent already.

'Dan, I'm worried – what if she never takes to us? What if this is as good as it gets?' I say to him. I'm genuinely worried.

'I'm worried too, but it's early days and I think that things will improve,' Dan says matter-of-factly.

I'm not sure if this is what he really believes or if he's trying to convince himself and me.

Monday 8 September 2014

Dan's left for work early as usual, and I drop Charlie off at school; I've been rattled by the weekend away, I can't deny it. I don't want to feel isolated and know that both Jessie and I will be stir-crazy if we don't start to mix with fellow mums and children, so I have decided to take her to a "rhythm and rhyme" session at a local children's centre.

When we enter the room, there are musical instruments all over the floor and chairs at the back of the room for parents to sit and chat. The age group is 0–2 years and there are quite a few tiny babies in car seats. Lots of the children Jessie's age are sitting on the floor playing with the instruments, and it's sad for me to watch the warm interaction between the other children and their mums or dads. I don't recognise any of the parents and strike up a conversation with a couple of mums who have daughters the same age as Jessie; their children are all walking and have a lot more hair than Jessie, who still looks like a beautiful young baby. 'Isn't she walking yet?' they ask me. 'No, not yet,' I reply, and can see them looking at Jessie.

'She hasn't got much hair, has she?' 'No, she hasn't got much hair,' I reply.

I can feel myself starting to get annoyed, so move away and play with Jessie instead. I didn't take Charlie to any of these sorts of groups because I went back to work when he was nine months old; I'm not sure I've made the right decision in coming now. I'm very protective of Jessie and don't like her being compared to other children; no one here knows the journey that she's been on and I'm not about to broadcast it to competitive mothers at a baby group.

Fortunately, the "rhyme" part of the session begins, and Jessie sits on the rug and watches the group leader sing; she wriggles around and starts to "dance". It's nice to see her enjoying herself. We all sing four or five nursery rhymes and then it's back to free play again. Jessie crawls off immediately and it's a job to keep up with her. She goes up to the tiny babies and pokes them; I remove her and take her back to the centre of the room, but she goes up to another baby, or another parent, or someone's handbag, or makes her way to the exit! I call her name but she doesn't react or come back to me; she's still not registering me as her mum.

On the way home, I decide that I'm not going to think about the future and what Jessie doesn't do yet, but will focus on the here and now and the things that she does do. She liked the nursery rhymes so I buy a CD of nursery rhymes for us to sing together at home. I walk for longer than I intended, trying to get things straight in my mind. I come to the conclusion that my mistake has been trying to force my mum status on Jessie. I need to let her take the lead, difficult and upsetting as that may be for me. I have to leave Jessie to come to terms with her new life in her own time. It's not about me and my feelings – it's about making sure that Jessie is OK. The affection and bond will come once she trusts us completely and feels safe. It's a cliché, but I'm going to take one day at a time, I'm going to think no further ahead than the present day. It's a sure-fire route to failure if I carry on worrying about the future.

Saturday 13 September 2014
I wake up with a feeling of dread; we've arranged to meet with Gwen, Jessie's foster carer, today. At the Life Appreciation Day, back in July, we agreed that we would meet up with Gwen again within three months of placement. Jessie had such a strong attachment to Gwen and hasn't transferred it to us yet, and I'm worried that she will reject us out of hand once she sees Gwen again.

I haven't seen Gwen since 29 July, when I ran out of her house and bundled Jessie into our car on that last day of introductions. We've spoken on the phone a couple of times but it's nervewracking to think that Jessie is going to see her again.

We've arranged to meet in the café where we took our breaks during introductions. Gwen is already there when we arrive and has another small baby with her in a pram. She greets us warmly with a huge grin, and gifts for Charlie and Jessie. Dan and I know that she wants to hold Jessie, so I pass her over and Gwen's face lights up.

'Oh, doesn't she look lovely! Hello Jessie, hello,' she says, bouncing Jessie on her knee; Jessie seems quite comfortable with Gwen but not as attached to her as she was before. I wonder what's going through her mind; she's so little and this must be very confusing for her. She's in a halfway house: she's friendly towards me, Dan and Gwen but not loving with any of us. Jessie wriggles around on Gwen's knee and we chat generally about how things have been over the last eight weeks, and while we chat Jessie puts Gwen's locket into her mouth, something she used to do when she lived with Gwen.

'Oh, she remembers me, do you think she does? She does, doesn't she, she remembers.' I take the opportunity to get a few photos of them together. It doesn't take long for Jessie to become fractious, however, and she starts to cry. Gwen tries to comfort her but this only seems to make Jessie cry even more. Charlie and I have tickets booked for the cinema later in the afternoon so we see this as probably the time to say goodbye to Gwen.

Meeting her again went better than I expected. I thought that it might be a little awkward, but Gwen was lovely and so pleased to see us that my worries were unfounded. It was good to see that Jessie didn't respond to Gwen any differently than to any of the "new" family members we've introduced her to lately, and it was a big positive that when she became upset with Gwen, she was happy to come back to me.

Sunday 14 September–October 2014

Charlie seems to be fine now that he's back at school; he's got his own friends and activities to distract him and give him an outlet, plus the fact that we've kept our promise to make time for just him alone. He's actually started to ask if Jessie can come along to the swimming sessions that he has with his dad. We're not sure how Jessie is going to take to the water, but she absolutely loves it! She splashes around with Charlie and it's a good way for us to get close skin-to-skin contact while I hold her in the pool. She clings on to me tightly – her little arms wrapped around my neck. It's a wonderful feeling and I can see that this will be a good way to help us to bond.

I've held back on the playgroups for now, as I feel they would put pressure on us both. I will re-join them when we are a stronger unit. I've had a few "Eureka" moments over the last week and it feels at last like we're starting to gel. Jessie was whining and miserable one afternoon and I was at the end of my tether, so I put some music on and scooped Jessie up in my arms and started to dance with her. She immediately stopped crying and we went on dancing like this for an hour or so. Whenever I tried to put her down, she put her arms up to me and wanted me to hold her and dance – another good way to get close!

Dan and I constantly talk and review how everyone is feeling and what's happening. We're very happy with how Charlie's coping, and after parents' evening with his new class teacher, I am able to relax a little where he is concerned. By sheer coincidence, his teacher has a six-year-old birth son and has adopted a two-year-old little girl. It's like a breath of fresh air to chat with him and to know that he's been in exactly the same situation as us. Charlie is delighted to know that he's not the only little boy to have adopted a sister and he is particularly happy to know that he can talk to his teacher if he needs to. Charlie has also had a hearing test at the hospital, which came back as inconclusive. He needs to repeat the test, but I think his holding of his ears and upset is a side effect of bringing Jessie into the family; once we get a definitive result we can begin to work through this with Charlie. It feels like things are slowly falling into place for us.

The visits from the social workers are fortnightly now, as agreed in the review meeting. Jessie has been allocated a new social worker who's visited a couple of times and is going to complete the court paperwork. This means that there shouldn't be any delays in our submission of documents to the court for our adoption order. We can't fault the support that we've had from our local authority. Before we began the process, we'd heard and read so many horror stories about missed appointments and delays that we couldn't help but fear the worst. However, we've been lucky with supportive social workers and an efficient authority.

Jessie's still not walking and although we're not overly concerned, Mandy, our social worker, pointed out that Jessie's foot seems to do something unusual when she crawls. I raise this with the health visitors at the next baby clinic and they tell me not to worry and that they'll have a look again once Jessie's walking. Mandy comments about the foot every time she visits, despite me relaying the health visitors' opinion. I talk to Dan about it as it feels like this small issue that we hadn't even noticed is being made into a big potential problem. Getting the attachment to work between Jessie and the rest of us is hard enough in itself without additional curveballs being thrown, which turn out to be insignificant. But we start looking at Jessie's foot and wondering if there might be something wrong with it after all. Dan tells me to take comfort from the health visitors' opinion and to put Mandy's concerns to the back of my mind – easier said than done! (Looking back, I think it would have been a good idea to get a second opinion, or at least to get advice from the agency medical adviser, just to stop us worrying.)

To add further pressure, we have to write letters to Jessie's birth mother and half-siblings this month. I'm happy to do so, but question why we have to write only two months after placement – it would make more sense to write our first letter in 2015. But we've signed the contract and agreed to the terms. I write a general letter about Jessie's birthday celebrations, her first holiday and her general likes and dislikes; it's easier to put together than I thought it would be. We only write one letter a year, in October, and then we wait and see if we receive a response. We've been told that Jessie's birth mother hasn't responded to letterbox contact with her other children, so realistically it's unlikely that we'll get a reply.

Jessie's met all of her new extended family now and is happy in their company. We're still very careful about visits to our house and try to limit them to an hour. This is Jessie's home territory now and we don't want her to feel confused. It's awkward at times; I've had to ask my mum and dad to leave when their visit overlapped with Jessie's dinner time – she wouldn't eat her dinner and started to become hyperactive, which is a sure sign that she's over-stimulated. I felt awful but I know Jessie and her behaviour now and I have to put her first, before extended family and friends' feelings or wishes – it's as simple as that.

Friday 24 October 2014
It's the second review meeting today and Charlie is at school this time. As well as the usual social workers, Jessie's health visitor is attending. The meeting is very relaxed, everyone's happy with how Jessie is coming along, so the review is almost a formality. We're asked if we want to proceed to court with the adoption order, and as we've prepared our part of the court paperwork in readiness for today, we say yes, yes, yes! It might be hard work and she may not have bonded with us fully yet, but Jessie is our daughter and Charlie's sister. I've relaxed into the belief that we just need to give ourselves time and space to adjust.

11

Learning to trust

OCTOBER 2014–MARCH 2015

Monday 27 October–Friday 31 October 2014

With the problems of our last holiday a not too distant memory, we've decided to book another break. The idea is to take Dan's mum, Jean, to visit one of her oldest friends, Joan, in Devon, and then carry on to have a couple of days on our own. It's only been, what, eight weeks since our weekend in Wales, but we're eternal optimists! Jessie seems to be more settled, and although not looking for affection, is happy to be held by us, and best of all, is pleased to see us in the morning when we lift her from her cot. This is not to imply that she's sleeping through the night – she most definitely is not. She wakes up three to four times, but when either Dan or I get her at 6am, she is always smiling and excited to see us, so that the night's events and the sleep deprivation are soon forgotten.

We collect Jean at around 9am and start our journey, and it's happily uneventful. Jessie has a little doze, so does Charlie, and we have to wake them up when we arrive at Joan's house. Joan used to be an emergency foster carer herself; we're lucky to have so many people close to us who we can talk to about adoption. Despite being eighty years old, Joan is active and energetic, so we're out of the house for a walk once Jean's bags have been unloaded from the car. The sea isn't too far away, and we walk down to the front and take photos of us all together, and Jessie is in a very good mood! And, dare I say it, I'm looking forward to our next few days away from home. I've been giving my all since the end of July – I'm really having to prove myself to this little person who has already been through so much in her young life.

We have a wonderful, carefree day with Joan before moving on to our accommodation for the next few nights. We've decided to stay at a holiday park with on-site entertainment for Charlie. The accommodation isn't great – a very small and basic apartment – but it's only a base from which to explore, so we can live with it for the next four nights.

We spend the days enjoying each other's company, walking along the beach and visiting little fishing villages along the coast in the October sunshine. Dan and I take it in turns to go out with Charlie at night; he loves the evening entertainment and wins prizes in a dance competition, of which he is extremely proud. On our third night, we are awoken just after midnight by a couple arguing in the apartment above us. They're in the bedroom directly above mine and Dan's, and as the walls are so thin, we can hear every word! The shouting goes on for half an hour or more and eventually wakes Jessie, who starts to cry. The couple must have heard her crying and move to a different room, where they continue to argue loudly for several hours! Eventually the park security team arrives and they quieten down, but by now it's early morning and we know that the children will be up soon. We agree that we won't spend another night here and will return home today.

Dan is sleepless and has the long drive home to look

forward to. We stop to see his mum and Joan on our way back.

It's such a shame – we were all having a good time, and for the first time Jessie seemed to enjoy being in a different environment – but we couldn't risk either of them being woken up again by doors slamming and shouting. Is something or somebody trying to tell us that holidays might not be a good idea just yet?

Saturday 1 November–Sunday 30 November 2014
November is very quiet for us all. Charlie's doing really well at school and I'm trying out a number of baby playgroups with Jessie. One of them has only two other children. As Jessie isn't walking yet, this leads to an interrogation by the other two mums. I eventually tell them that Jessie is adopted, and immediately regret it because another round of intrusive questioning follows. Mandy has told me that there are courses available to help adopters to deal with other people's questions, and I can see why they are needed. It's as though it's open season and no question is off limits! Strangers think it's OK to ask why Jessie was adopted, what happened to her birth mother; they feel that they can ask, 'Was it neglect?' while regarding Jessie sympathetically, or, 'Isn't it wonderful that you've adopted her; will you tell her she's adopted?', and even, 'Is Charlie adopted too?'. I hate telling other parents that Jessie is adopted and then watching them look at her differently. I prefer either to change the subject or to answer vaguely. Jessie is a fifteen-month-old baby and to the outside world I want her to be like any other fifteen-month-old baby – Dan and I will make sure that she knows how and why she joined our family and about her past. We have had numerous discussions and agree that details about Jessie's birth parents are to be kept to ourselves because this is Jessie's personal and private information. Yes, we will reveal that she's adopted, but the details are for her ears only.

If at a later stage she feels that she wants to share what she knows with others, then that's Jessie's choice. And for the record: Jessie's the one who's transformed our lives, not the other way round.

I've decided that I'll run my own private playgroup at home with just me and Jessie until after Christmas. I buy lots of puzzle games and craft supplies and we have nursery rhymes playing in the background – I've finally managed to wean Jessie off television during the day. She loves action rhymes and nods her head to the music or wriggles around, and after a few sessions she comes to sit on my lap to sing 'Incy wincy spider' or 'Row, row, row the boat'. I love this, it's the first time that she's come to me on her own and got close. I'm naturally affectionate so it gives me a good excuse to cuddle her and she doesn't pull away. I'm not sure if she doesn't know how to cuddle or whether she's not sure about cuddling me, so we role-play with her teddy bears. I cuddle them and say, 'Ahhh, it's a baba,' and she copies me, saying, 'Aaah, baba'. I think I've done the right thing by not joining playgroups at this point, in spite of being asked about it by the social workers during their monthly visits (after the second review it was agreed that we would have monthly visits until the adoption hearing). I know that it's vitally important for Jessie to socialise with other children, but I want us to have formed a closer bond before we bring other children and locations into the equation, and we can only do that by spending time together one-on-one.

Monday 1 December–Wednesday 31 December 2014

December is pretty much like November – quiet. The cold winter weather means that we can't get out as much as we'd like and we're more or less waiting for Christmas to come – at least once you get to 21 December, you can take some comfort that lighter mornings and evenings are on their way.

I go Christmas shopping with Dan's mum and Jessie, and whilst in one of the large department stores decide to take Jessie to see Father Christmas, as there isn't a queue. It's a lovely grotto, with mechanical reindeer and people dressed up as elves. When we reach Father Christmas' office, I take Jessie inside and hand her over to him for a photo; she takes one look at him and SCREAMS! I quickly take her back and try to console her, but she just doesn't like the look of him and the photo that we have is of her crying her eyes out. Oh dear, I thought she might like it but I'm going by our experience with Charlie, who wasn't fazed at all when we took him to see Santa at a similar age.

In December, Dan and I also have our first night out together since Jessie's placement. As we both work in finance, we often used to laugh that we only ever go out "quarterly", but neither of us has had the slightest inclination to go out during the last five months – we've been too exhausted. We decide to celebrate Christmas with a meal out and leave Dan's mum with babysitting duties. We enjoy a good chat, Italian food and a few cocktails, knowing that if the children wake up they are in Jean's capable hands. We return home around 10pm (we don't want to push it – we don't know what we're coming back to). Jean tells us that she hasn't heard a peep from Jessie and that she and Charlie watched a bit of TV together before he settled to sleep.

Jessie has started to sleep through some nights – not every night, but when we wake up in the mornings and realise that we've both had a full night's uninterrupted sleep, we feel like doing a victory dance around the bedroom. You don't know how important a good night's sleep is until you don't have it! Some nights, however, Jessie decides that she's going to wake us four times.

We've booked Charlie a visit to see Father Christmas at a local garden centre and take Jessie with us. We love this magical time of year. We all enter the cabin to see Father

Christmas and Jessie starts to cry again. She's in her pushchair so I wheel her out away from Scary Santa.

Thursday 25 December 2014: Christmas Day
Christmas morning has finally arrived. Charlie wakes up at 5.30am and finds his stocking at the end of his bed full of treats and chocolate; he knows that Father Christmas has been and bursts into our room to tell us the good news. Jessie hears the commotion and wakes up too, so we lead the way and take the children downstairs. They are very lucky and the floor is covered with presents. Charlie's face is a picture, he's ridiculously excited. He doesn't waste much time in tearing open his presents and is very grateful for all the lovely gifts from family and friends. Jessie is a little more cautious: she sits on Dan's knee and watches Charlie and it's the quietest I've seen her – she can't have any clue about what's happening. Once Charlie has finished opening his presents, we ask him to help Jessie with hers, which he happily agrees to do. When Jessie sees Peppa Pig toys, she starts to become a little more interested and involved in tearing the paper from the gifts. She's still a little subdued and I'm worried how the day and visitors are going to affect her.

Dan's mum is coming to our house for Christmas dinner this year. She did offer to make other arrangements, as it's our first year with Jessie, but we want her to join us. It's funny though – just lately Jessie has become very upset when she sees not only Jean, but if she is spoken to or approached by anyone with an "older" face. She does calm down eventually but woe betide if Jean tries to touch her. It's the only time that Jessie clings to me and it's nice to be able to provide comfort.

My mum, dad and nan come to the house at 10am and stay for an hour, just until Dan's mum arrives. It works out well. There aren't too many people in the house at the same time so Jessie doesn't get over-stimulated and hyperactive.

Christmas lunch is a joint effort, but unfortunately this means that one of us in in the kitchen while the other is entertaining guests, so we don't have much time to enjoy the day as a family. Dan's brother and niece pop in later in the morning and I'm able to get a couple of nice photos of Amy and Jessie together; Charlie is off with his uncle playing with his new toy gun in the garden and doesn't want to be photographed. We have a relaxed lunch and remaining day, but like most households at Christmas we eat far too much.

The best bit about the Christmas period is that Dan is at home for almost two weeks, and I'm really looking forward to this time together. We don't do much of anything, just enjoy family time and see the New Year in together. We're both feeling positive about the future and Jessie sleeps through the night – a promising start to 2015?

Thursday 1 January–Saturday 31 January 2015
There is a flurry of activity from the social workers as the deadline for them to submit their reports to court is 29 January, and they want to make sure that they have got all of the information they need to avoid any delays.

Charlie has his second hearing test at the hospital and is given the all clear – nothing wrong with his hearing at all. I'm relieved; I hated the thought that he might be suffering pain or not able to hear properly. At least now we know that he simply finds Jessie's crying far too loud. He hasn't been upset about the noise for some time now; he's used to Jessie being around and they are developing a lovely relationship. Jessie absolutely adores her big brother and it's lovely to hear them playing and laughing.

Jessie is pulling herself up but isn't walking yet and I'm not sure whether to be worried or not. I can see how frustrated she is getting and want to be able to help her. Whenever I visit the baby clinic, I mention my concern about her not walking and ask whether there could be something wrong with her foot, but I'm told that it wouldn't even be looked at unless Jessie is not walking at two years old. Dan and I decide that we have no option but to wait, as we've been told.

We've received a reply from Jessie's half-brother's adoptive family in response to our letter to them. I'm a little worried as he seems to have all sorts of developmental issues including dyspraxia, and I wonder if Jessie may have this too and that's why she's not walking yet. I read everything I can about this condition and find that children with dyspraxia have shoes that are built up around the ankle to offer more support. We've bought Jessie some shoes but they are like little ballet pumps and offer no support whatsoever. Dyspraxia or not, I figure that it can't hurt to buy her some shoes with more ankle support and that it might help her to walk. If this doesn't work, we'll have to seek the doctor's help.

I need to keep a closer eye on Jessie anyway, as she had a strange reaction to something at Dan's mum's house earlier in the week. Jean has some Christmas ornaments around the fireplace and one of them plays a tinkly Christmas song; as soon as Jessie heard it she threw herself onto her back on the floor and completely froze, staring upwards into space. I picked her up and it was about ten minutes before she calmed down enough to want me to put her down – a very unusual reaction! I mention it to our social worker, and she tells me that she could have had a "silent seizure". I instantly research this and find that they take place in children from the age of four. I have a different theory – it sounds a bit odd but I think that the sound reminds her of being at her foster carer's house. I also think that is why Jessie gets upset by older faces. Dan's mum is a double whammy because she wears gold chains just like Gwen. I wonder if Jessie worries that she might be moving again when she sees or hears these "triggers". Obviously she can't tell us, but her extreme reaction to certain sounds or people is strange indeed.

I raise our concern at the baby clinic, but I'm told not to worry. The health visitor tells me that babies do just decide to cry at certain people and that it's unfortunate it's my mother-in-law – it's a stage and Jessie will grow out of it. I also mention the dyspraxia but again am told that there wouldn't be any type of investigation until Jessie is two years old. The health visitor is very reassuring. Dan and I consider whether we should get a second opinion, but think that this would probably lead to the same outcome – that we'll have to wait until Jessie is two years old.

Sunday 18 January 2015
It's Dan's mum's birthday and we've been invited for a family carvery. I have to put Jessie first and tell Dan that Jessie and I won't be able to come. Jean is upset and questions Dan, but he is in full agreement with me. Jessie isn't interested in eating much at the moment; she doesn't like sitting in a high chair; she throws finger food on the floor, and won't eat cooked food unless it's blended. She will tolerate some lumps but won't eat solid food. I know what the outcome will be if we take her to a crowded restaurant and expect her to eat meat and veg. Jessie needs to be used to eating out with me, Dan and Charlie in a quieter environment before we can think about these sorts of family events.

Dan's brother tells Jean, 'Amy used to scream and cry in restaurants but we still took her.' I've not made the decision because I'm embarrassed by Jessie's crying – I had a thick skin before we adopted and I certainly don't care what a bunch of strangers in a restaurant think of us – it's Jessie I'm protecting.

Wednesday 21 January 2015
We have a visit from the health visitor, which Dan takes care of, as I'm at a conference in London with my employer. It's nice to get my work clothes on and spend a

day with my colleagues. I'd forgotten what it's like to have adult conversation – it's wonderful to escape and be something other than a mum for the day.

I call Dan when I can, to see how Jessie's health assessment has gone, and he tells me that although she has improved in some areas, she is behind in others. Well, it doesn't come as much of a surprise to me as she isn't walking and that's going to be a huge milestone to reach. We knew that there was a good chance that Jessie might regress or not develop as you would expect due to the stress of moving from foster care, but it's still difficult to take. None of the professionals we have spoken to are concerned – they tell us to wait and assure us that she'll soon catch up. Jessie is alert, inquisitive and intelligent, she is brilliant at building with her blocks, at doing puzzles and has started to hold a pencil well – she just won't walk.

Thursday 29 January 2015
Jessie has taken her first steps – I'm so proud of her that I could explode.

The new shoes seem to have done the trick and have given her that little bit of extra confidence. It happened this evening and Dan, Charlie and I were all there to witness it. I see how pleased she is with herself and scoop her up and run around the room with her shouting, 'Hooray – clever girl!' We wonder whether it's a one-off, but sure enough, she continues to toddle around the living room chasing after Charlie. The thought that she could be behind developmentally that has been in the backs of our minds recedes. Jessie just does things in her own time, not to a schedule.

Sunday 1 February–Saturday 28 February 2015

Monday 16 February 2015
It's half-term again for Charlie and he wants to get his

50 metres swimming badge. I have Jessie with me, Dan is at work and I'm not sure how I'm going to manage. I'll have my hands full trying to keep Jessie out of the water but I desperately want to watch Charlie swim. I know that there's some sort of playroom at the leisure centre where the swimming pool is, and we ask what time it opens. I find out that it's a council-run crèche and that I can leave Jessie for the two hours that Charlie is scheduled to swim. I have a look around and can see that the other children look happy playing with the staff, so complete the necessary forms. 'I'm just at the swimming pool,' I tell them. If there are any problems I'm in the same building and can be reached very quickly.

It feels weird not to have Jessie with me but it's a complete relief that I can concentrate on Charlie and give him my full support to get his swimming badge. He swims his 50 metres beautifully and I give him a massive well done bearhug before taking him for a nice cup of hot chocolate at the coffee shop. We pick Jessie up earlier than we thought and the helpers tell me that she absolutely loved the crèche and had loads of fun with the other children. I call Dan and tell him the good news. Charlie's Street Dance class is held in this leisure centre and we will now be able to watch him dance and know that Jessie is happily playing. Stumbling on this by sheer accident has cured so many headaches for us and also allows Jessie to start to socialise with other children of her age.

Thursday 26 February 2015
After the success at the leisure centre crèche, I get in touch with the local Children's Centre to find that they run a two-hour playgroup for children without their parents/carers, and as luck would have it, there is a place that Jessie can have if we want – of course we want! There are ten other children in the group, all of them over eighteen months old. I take Jessie in and she runs off

straight away to play with the toys and the other children. She isn't bothered when I leave her. I've now got two precious hours to do what I want. I catch up with some cleaning, with one eye on my phone waiting for a call from the playgroup, but there isn't one.

When I return to collect Jessie two hours later, I see the other children running up to the gate with their little arms out, shouting 'Mummy'. Jessie hasn't said Mummy or Daddy yet, she babbles a lot but not words that can be understood. I'm so pleased to see her but a tiny bit sad that I don't get that same greeting. Nevertheless, I get a nice smile and she doesn't cry when I pick her up.

The women who run the playgroup give me a leaflet about a swimming club on a Friday morning and I instantly sign us up and look forward to the first session in March.

Sunday 1 March–Sunday 29 March 2015

Friday 6 March 2015

Jessie and I drop Charlie off at school and make our way to the swimming pool for our first session. There's to be 45 minutes in the water followed by an hour of play. The pool is wonderfully warm when we step in and it's a proper swimming lesson with a qualified teacher. Jessie is very comfortable and we enjoy the time in the water together, which mainly consists of singing nursery rhymes! It's a precursor to formal swimming lessons with children in the pool alone. It helps to get babies used to being in the water and to getting their faces splashed a little. If Jessie could talk, she'd be telling me how much she likes this, I can tell by her smiley, happy face, and she lets me hold her close while she laughs and splashes in the water.

I dry her off and take her down to the room where the children will play. She stands in the middle of the room and screams with her arms reaching out to me, letting me know in no uncertain terms that she doesn't want to be here. I gather her up and we leave and she calms immediately. I wonder if she is worried that I'll leave her and she doesn't want to be separated from me after the nice time we've had in the pool. That would be something quite new.

Friday 13 March 2015
A solar eclipse is due to plunge us into darkness at precisely 10am, and coincidentally at 10am it is the first part of the court process to adopt Jessie. It is the birth parent hearing – an opportunity for Jessie's birth mother to contest the decision for us to adopt her. The social workers don't think that Jessie's birth mother will attend as she hasn't submitted any papers to court to indicate that she will; however, I can't help but worry.

Jessie and I are at our swimming group and we watch the sky darken a little through the windows of the pool; it's not quite the descent into darkness we've been told to expect but you can see that the sun has disappeared. Jessie's social worker has assured me that she will call as soon as she has finished at court, so all I can do is enjoy the swim and wait for the call to come. Then Jessie has a sleep and I watch Comic Relief on TV until mid-afternoon. I can't concentrate to read or do anything else. At around 2pm I can't bear it any longer, and text Jessie's social worker to see how things are going. She replies that she's just left court and that the birth mother didn't show up. I'm incredibly relieved; in twenty-eight days' time, we should have an adoption hearing and Jessie will legally be our daughter.

12

Into the future

FROM MARCH 2015

Monday 30 March–Friday 3 April 2015
Yet another few days by the sea in Wales, and this time we've risked staying a little longer than before. It's Charlie's Easter holiday from school and Dan and I are very aware that summer was boring for him and we're trying to make it up to him. We're also hoping to create as many good memories of Jessie's first year with us as we can. When we arrive the weather is horrendous, it's bitterly cold and extremely windy and it doesn't look much like improving. The first thing we do when we get to the shops is buy woolly hats. It's not enjoyable for Jessie, and although we stay together for the first night, Dan decides to take Jessie back home and leave me and Charlie to spend time together.

We miss them both but it's quite an adventure: we explore the local area, walk along the beach, take a bus further along the coast, go to the theatre, and swim. It's the first time Jessie and I have been apart since July, but it's wonderful for me and Charlie to have an adventure together. It's good for Dan and Jessie too, to have time together alone. We talk every night by video call and she's always smiling when she sees us and seems to be enjoying her time with her dad. I am really enjoying the peace and the ability to have a conversation with Charlie without having to dash off to tend to Jessie; I hadn't realised until I was away from her just how much she whinges and cries – it's been a constant background noise that I've simply become accustomed to.

Dan comes to pick us up on Good Friday and we spend the day together on the promenade, eating freshly cooked doughnuts and drinking hot chocolate. When we get home that afternoon, I put Jessie to bed for her usual nap and I'm so happy to hold and hug her – I've really missed her. Jessie, on the other hand, is very upset with me and screams as loud as she can and thrashes around her cot. I pick her up again and she hits out at me, twisting and turning away from me so that I have to put her back in the cot. She doesn't want me there at all and is hysterical. I leave her in the cot for her own safety. This takes me straight back to the start of the placement. Eventually she lies on her front and I stroke her back and try to pacify her. She lies very still, and is quiet, and allows me to carry on like this for about five minutes. Then, without warning, she stands up and starts babbling and laughing and putting her arms out for me to pick her up as though the last twenty minutes had never happened. I understand that she was angry with me for leaving her and is communicating in the only way she can. When I pick her up, she holds me tight for a good few minutes with her head resting on my shoulder; it's then that I realise how much I love her.

I've read books and listened to social workers talk about how your adopted child will "grow in your heart", and I now understand what this means. Up until now I cared for Jessie and wanted to look after her, but now I know that I love her as much, and in the same way, as I love Charlie. It was easier for Dan: he loved Jessie from the minute we brought her home with us; it just wasn't the same for me and I struggled with my feelings. I carried Charlie and loved him while he was growing inside me; when he was born and I held him for the first time I knew that I'd never felt love like it and it was instantly reciprocated. Charlie was comforted by me being near, looked for affection, was excited to see me. Having been so lucky, I was very worried when I didn't immediately feel like this when Jessie came to us. I have felt very guilty and cried about not really loving her, but I think I was being too hard on myself. I gave Jessie the time and space to get used to me and to learn to love me, so why did I think that it was wrong to give time and space to myself?

It's a wonderful point to get to and I feel, after eight months, that we've finally "attached" and bonded with one another. When I collect her from her Wednesday afternoon playgroup, she runs up to the gate at last with her arms out to me, and when I pick her up, she rests her head on my shoulder; I can feel the tears in my eyes and can't wait to tell Dan.

Tuesday 14 April 2015
This is the day that we've been waiting for – the celebration court hearing when we legally adopt Jessie. After today we will have full parental responsibility for Jessie – and no more visits from social workers!

Dan and I had wanted to keep the court hearing very low-key with just us, Jessie and Charlie. It was going to be a formality for us; she is already a member of our family. When we let Dan's mum know that we have a court date at last, 'I'm coming to that', she tells us, so of course we invite my parents along too.

For Charlie, the day is extra-special as he should be at school but has been allowed a day off by his head teacher. The school was wonderfully supportive when I contacted them. They agree that it is vitally important for us to all be able to attend court today and legally acknowledge the four of us as a family unit.

Charlie's particularly excited about meeting a judge, especially since he knows that it's not something all six-year-olds are able to do.

'Do judges send people to jail?' Charlie asks.

'Well, yes, judges do send people to jail but we're going to a family court today,' I reply.

'Will there be any robbers or bad guys there?' It is a combined criminal and family court so there might well be. I think Charlie has been watching too many superhero films lately but decide against saying so.

'No, Charlie, there won't be any bad guys, just us, the social workers and the judge,' I finally reply.

Everyone comes to our house and we travel to court in a convoy in order to arrive together. On the outskirts of the city, just a couple of miles away from the court, we see a car parked in the middle of the road with the driver apparently slumped in his seat. We carry on past but Dan decides to pull over a little further up the road to see if help is needed. I know we have to help but I'm also thinking, 'We'd better not be late – it's a huge day for us!' My dad pulls over too and Dan and I and my dad run back to where the car is parked to see if the driver is OK. But the car isn't there any more! We come to the conclusion that the driver must have fallen asleep at the wheel. Bit of an odd one, but at least there's no emergency for us to deal with so we run all the way back to the car to continue on our way to the court. My dad assures us that he knows how to get to the city centre and that he and my mum will see us there.

The court is a huge building with security screening at the entrance. I watch Charlie as he gazes around open-mouthed; I can see his imagination running away with him. We go through the double doors that lead to the family court and see Mandy and Penny, our social workers, already there and waiting. It's lovely to see them again and we greet each other like long-lost friends. The clerk of the court asks us if everyone is here and it's then I realise that my mum and dad haven't arrived. I call my mum and she tells me that they got lost and are about five minutes away from the court. I'm mortified that we have to ask the clerk to hold the hearing; at this moment I can't imagine anything worse than keeping a judge waiting!

I'm in and out of the building, ringing my mum to see where they are until fifteen minutes after the court hearing should have started, when they finally arrive.

'I won't be back again,' I say to the security guard at the entrance.

'That's what they all say,' he replies, making me laugh and lightening the mood instantly.

Finally we can go into the courtroom and the judge enters; it's all very informal and she doesn't wear the usual wig and gown but a navy blue suit. She has a second judge with her whom she is training; 'Two for the price of one,' she quips before explaining how she very much enjoys this part of her job, that she's read all of the court papers relating to Jessie and is delighted that she will be legally joining our family. The judge asks Charlie to introduce everyone, which he does beautifully. We are congratulated and given the paperwork showing that Jessie now carries our surname. The judge then invites me to sit in her chair with the family around me while we have photos taken. It's a lovely moment.

We celebrate the event with a meal in a restaurant near the court and are delighted at how well Jessie copes; even, dare I say it, how much she enjoys the situation.

In the eyes of the law, Jessie is now our daughter, and this is the start of her new life as a member of our family. We won't let Jessie forget where she came from or how she came to us, but it's such a good feeling to know that we're moving forward together as a family of four. Jessie has a mum, a dad and a big brother who adore her.

What does the future hold for us? Well, in the short term, we've booked a christening for Jessie and are looking forward to celebrating with a big party for all of our friends and family.

Long term, it's not a fairy tale and there's no miracle ending. We're just a normal family and will go on having the same worries and problems as any other family. Jessie's delay in walking and eating has made us realise that we can't take anything for granted in regard to her development. We just have to wait, watch and react if we feel worried at any stage, but we won't worry any more or any less than we do about Charlie. I feel privileged to be able to watch Charlie and Jessie grow up together to develop their own characters and personalities and to call them my children; that's a good enough future for me.

September 2015

It's over a year since Jessie came to live with us and five months since the adoption order was granted. I've returned to work, so Jessie attends a nursery close to our house, which she absolutely loves. When we arrive in the morning, she rushes in to her keyworker full of smiles. The interaction with other children and the wide and varied daily activities have brought her development on in leaps and bounds.

Jessie now feels able to show us affection and often comes to me, Dan or Charlie with outstretched arms asking for a cuddle. We still have moments when Charlie feels as though Jessie gets more attention than he does, but this is more in line with "normal" sibling rivalry and we explain that Jessie is only two years old and can't do a lot of things for herself yet. Jessie adores her big brother and has the attitude that "whatever he can do, I can do". She wants the same drinks as him, and to eat exactly the same food as him and she loves it when they chase each other around the lounge. She often copies Charlie and calls us

Mum and Dad, rather than Mummy and Daddy as most toddlers do.

However, my favourite moment so far was when Dan, Charlie and Jessie came to pick me up from work one evening. I walked out of the building to be greeted by Charlie, who ran into me, almost knocking me over, and hugged me. Dan had Jessie on reins, but when she caught sight of me, she shouted with happiness and ran towards me with her little arms out and the biggest smile on her face, dragging Dan behind her, and shouting, 'Mummy, Mummy, Mummy, Mummy!' When she finally reached me, she jumped for me to pick her up. My little girl in my arms and my little boy cuddling my waist – there is no better feeling than this. This is Dan's and my family. Everything has been worth it for moments like this.

BC	02/17